GW01606583

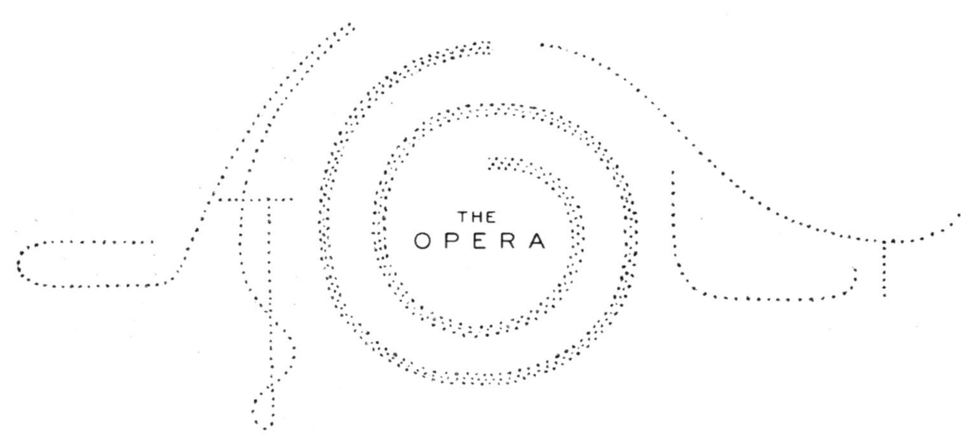

THE
OPERA

Contents

RHEA DILLON

CATGUT

LIBRETTO

OVERTURE

Finding Response to Masque of Blackness' Lingua Franca:

Here lies a conceit that foreshadows the magnanimous tyrant who though but black in face
is yet bright and full of life and light.
To prove that beauty best, which, not the colour, but the feature assures unto the creature.

I possess an immortal soul of creatures mortal. I run through many trunks and carve many lives in the breast of concentric direction.

This squared circle of celestial bodies

in the breast of concentric direction.

To be as fair as death means to be born of its pale faithful hue to decay so free and quick linear strikes eyes, jaw and lip southward.

Weakened by concentric direction.

Virtue though chained to earth must live free and hell itself must seep over industry.

I rest scorched and seek intemperate fires.
Circumfused with light that would only boil the pale.
Born of this heat our blood never settles to mere stream
but races to read mystic lines.
My trouble is I seek nowness when old is the richest pure.
Old is the gold against silver star spangled worktops and chopping blocks.
When fluids turn to bleach
run to bathe in nearest ocean
corking ears to revive the corpse they seek to turn you into,
and salve the rude defects of their creature.
When you emerge,
know safety awaits
for the sun indeed refines all things
her radiance shines with warmth and love from her
black gaze, the colour shall be restored upon your face.

Now as per tradition this scene must be destroyed after the revels
to never again be performatised.

ACT 1 / ESSAY

This is an opera of the street.

This is an opera that will act as an antithetical with exponential drift.

This is an opera that means it and everything I do is in opposition to something.

The something being the consistently growing worldwide alt right government
and capitalocene.

This opera as exponential drift will involve the antithetical as its exponent
so when you hear the libretto its value will increase over time, after time.

An opera of the street because my favourite thing is sound.
How do you compose a sound?
Displace compose
How do you script a sound?
Displace the sound
How do you write for performance the questions in the air?
By re-engaging with the questionnaire as the base form for performance I have
questions that I myself can answer but must pose to the state as the state must
change. Social reconfiguration must penetrate the institutional mindset
and I beg to call forth my performance as critical engagement
with the black performing body always having been a performing body
from its entry into the Western world
underlying the quotidian of any black performing body.
As performances work as symbols for the subject matter, does this make my piece
a symbol of a symbol?
Am I Prince?
Perhaps a prince, perhaps more pronce.

Irregardless,
it doesn't matter who these people are. What they represent in clothing or colour.
They are parts of a piece of art, which is part of an artist performance series, in
an art gallery right here right now. This gallery is one of the most progressive
contemporary institutions in London. Front facing wise. That's what you came to see.
A front facing experience. A show. You expect, and hope, that when you leave this
pavilion-parked gallery your perception of what art can be will be altered, perhaps
even expanded, even if by the fact
you now know another human making art, or saw another way in which someone
can label something as art.
In my limited experience of happiness, you would like to have your reference of
good art confirmed, disrupted or violated by the art you see here.
Feel here: Hear here.
Smell here.
You would like a full body experience from a single utterance.
You would like to tell your friends, colleagues, peers

of the wonder you felt at the wonderful work you did see-feel-hear-smell.
You look forward to being challenged by this art to see things around you in an aesthetically heightened way. It's clear, you want something and 'exciting' to think about, to not be bored or antagonised.

You want to have an out-of-body experience. You want the bodies outside of you to introduce you to the 9th wonder of the world
or at least the explanation of the journey the artist took to get them there. A story telling of the struggle and plight.

[l o n g   p a u s e]

Instead, you got the loop. No-thing. Catgut.
Catgut. A no-thing.

[l o n g   p a u s e]

A moment for historical reference. You were here,

[p a u s e]

even if you left by the second act, a clocking occurred between you and your kin. This clocking wasn't to be kind, it was with intention; we see each other. And right now, we do not. Artist and you do not see each other. You never have. That was a privilege before. It will cost you now. As it will always cost the artist to be present. In the body they inhabit, showing up doesn't exist. Only showing out prevails. There is a weight in 'out' that cannot be calculated; only felt.
Cannot be described; only implied.

The preceding speaks in the present tense of the artist not being present.

The following speaks of what not being present means in regards to a performer.

[p a u s e]

Refusing to stand before you promotes a refusal of one's own perception, yet these are the artist's words, thoughts, emotions, grievances, propaganda, criticisms, claims and whimsy. In this duality of supposed oxymoronic 'present absence' they, the artist, thinks of what Bryan Wagner calls 'existence without standing'. From no light to stand in, no stage to gaze up over, a desire emerges in the navigation of daily performing to black performance
into this presentism performa.

Hartman states: 'The relationship between Blackness and performance is mediated through sets of prohibitions and permissions... The appearance and embodiment of blackness does not reveal a fixed, essential or evidential 'certainty' of the black body, but rather folds back onto the stability of the category of performance itself'.
When I, the artist, reads 'no certainty of the black body' I see the duppy in the daily.
I see the staging of the barely standing.

So [l o n g   p a u s e] where do you stand on the stage of it all?

Sometimes you just need a long journey to the edge of your mind to annihilate a fear. Fear feels like a strong word but, between my therapist and I, fear has been circumcised in its glory to become instead: 'Face Everything And Rise'. It now joins the only other slogan I've memorised that rightfully comes from my grandma: 'If you don't ask you don't get' (or 'the answer will always be no' [I like the always here as potent reminder so interchange the endings at will]). These two phrases coexist without asking.
Without displacing fear you never get anything.
Nothing is true desire. Because part of the desired is to be attractive.
But 'attractive' in that it is yet to be attained - is it out of reach?
A bridge and thus a path induced fear always exists.
In bridging this gap of
me to subject,
or,
as subject to object, I've been asking the question:

What does it mean to make a performance as a black person when the black body has always and is always performing?

But first one must start with:

Who can reframe Black performance without creating more pain from its reperformed enactment?

I grapple with whether Hartman tells us the answer here:
'The very spector of enjoyment is reason enough to repress the encounter'
Or if Moten tells us the answer here:
'One asks if every recitation is a repression and if every reproduction of a performance is its disappearance... the conjunction of reproduction and disappearance is performance's condition of possibility, its ontology and its mode of production'

If it's the former then it's clear the threat of enjoyment of the spectacle aka the performance itself is why or how to avoid the decision for a repeated black performance.

If it's the latter, we are always stuck in the radical breakdown.

'Is there a way to subject this unavoidable model of subjection to a radical breakdown?'

The radical breakdown is the loop. No-thing. Catgut.
Catgut. A no-thing.

Black sensibilities—the enlivened, vibrating components of a palpable black familiar—demonstrate the microeconomics of gesture that cohere in black performance.
Black performance contains history and racism, but it is not about either of those things.
Black performance is not static, contained, or geographically specific.
The very notion of capital B 'Black', however, is conceived within political/social economies of power defined by historical circumstances.
Black performance injects itself into pertinent political discussions like those surrounding the death of Stephen Lawrence, Mark Duggan or more recently Dea-John Reid.
Markings associated with black performance—such as brown to Black skin tones, or a hoodie—can be deadly. The killing of Duggan as well as those in the US like Trayvon Martin demonstrate this.
Clearly, theorising black performance is imperative in the present moment.

Theory does the labour of translating the thick ontologies of what Black imperatives are by locating them within the generative forces of performance.

Where is the analysis of black performance in the mundane quotidian?

In queering the capacities of theoretical intervention we arrive at the urgency in this work. What is this work on this occasion to us?

This is encapsulated in my questioning: What is the difference between a reading and a performance?

It's natural to instinctively exclaim 'there isn't one!'
but that would be a lie.
I know it.
We know it.
The difference lies between the following structures: delivery, context, audience, time and staging.

Delivery because such a thing as a 'story reading voice' is at liberty to be switched on or mimicked to pertain to the institutionalisation of oral language used for commanding space. For example, heard at town hall meetings or your local/global leader conference. Both follow an ideology of proper English stemming from a

Shakesperian rhythm. Also, note the physical delivery: is there gesticulation or moves to the piece?

So which is this?

Context because framework can flip the script: is it dialogue, is it prose, is it poetry, is it poetics, is it poethics…

So which is this?

Audience because 'are the members of the public classed as an audience or followers? Audience as a traditionally older sibling of following. Following as in Rihanna and her Navy.
Art performance is a space for release of emotions and trials: shared not entertained, offered not projected.
Music has audience and followers, but art performance has just audience and their desire.
Sound comes before body in musical performance.
Body comes before sound in art performance.

So which is this?

Time because as performance, we could be here for hours. But I wouldn't do that to you.

So which is this?

Staging because this is simple: if you have a single mic and are reading off an iPhone notes app this is the modern day edgy 'just wrote this on the train here and thought why not share it with you tonight since we're being open' stage code of a reading. Sometimes no mic, ode to the soapbox era.
If a point has been made to alter the naked permanent stage or space, an inference of performance is heightened. The way the body is staged (here best termed as costumed) is also a sign.
Mundane art scene dress doesn't cut it to be a performance.

So WHAT is this?

This is where performance meets its maker.

ACT 2 / POEM

One is either capable of becoming an actor or not; if not, then one is consumed by death.
- I won't even mention the priests!

[p a u s e]

That is why I say: an Orator is a dictating model, but dictated by Nothing. Which means not dictating at all by himself. And ultimately, to know how to kill oneself, that is to exist without risking injury to another.

The pure expression of man's greatness can be voiced in opera for man consents to listen to himself in his veracity.
But do we still need the stage to see greatness, one should ask?
Don't we see it in the mirror of society's chance meetings?
But that's nonsense, for opera is not a convention but a necessary organ.
You want to make of opera a pure and simple convention as one only gives to numbers a digit value.
That is a remarkable mistake.

If beauty on the waters stood, I don't read with you following fingers.
I draw a line and share from there.
Seek from there:

[p a u s e]

It feels like everything ends with fire. But what if the flame was where we begun.
licked most pure,
christened in heat pellets scold skin for a new anewing,
white as the ash of black flesh after flame.
So what after.
Take away burning affect,
speak to the layer left,
blanket weighted.
Who feeds us to clear this new beginning?
Dust off the leaves
spit, clean, rubbed, bark edge.
What's water anyway but fire if it hurts you?
Tongue to tongue quick whips
and you're equally through.
A feast of blue and black at breaking ground,
an orgy for some future perfect genius willing to start today.
It's not too late.
The ash will only pile up as we wait.
It's not too late.

[p a u s e]

It is, however, so much harder to jump from a pendulum. Self squashing writhing holding and releasing,
excreting with a tampon is the closest it comes.
Self preservation is what's really going on today.
Raking it in baby - baby I can't stroke you whilst I fuck you and the state, there aren't enough fingers to thumbs.
Only this once because it's your 30th and we'll be dead to the world's eye
by the next candlelight celebration.
Finger follows the lined.
Alone with the 'in mourning' pieces of you I wriggle into the light to expose the shapes of my carapace forever and ever.
What an enchanting tortoise I will be.

Let me see you from inside your formation. Raise the horse breath, light broken
on back of centaurs who've only known labour. Laid bare four footed figurines gallop on the inside of my stomach,
up under my breast, into the throat cavity. Lay, rinse–here it's densely packed with people I wish to speak to but cannot find the words.
I, site of dirt.
I sutured generation of the gaping past beauty
breathing still breathing fire onto the dehiscent
borders,
boundaries
and territories.

[p a u s e]

Terrorised villains, if blackness was no longer stable, what are its performative markers? Blackness as marker of simultaneously both the performance of the object and the performance of humanity.

If it probes its own distortion in your crystal, make it wait.
If it pierces the wind that flew shards into your spirit, make it wait.
Do Angels have shadows? How many Daemons can dance on the head of a pin?

If we're asking about Angels they don't dance they float.
If you're asking, it should be about the Daemons,
their feet be stomping, stay stomping on my grave.
Another day ready for the grave.

[p a u s e]

This is not an opera this is an omen
This is not an opera this is a sermon
This is not an opera this is a spiritual
This is not an opera this is a room to claim as one's own. No not yours Becky,
Karen, Susan,
Billy, Ken, Graham,
Jenny, Kelly, Carol,
Joe, Michael, Alan,
Jane, Katie, Liv, Sarah, Tanya—no,
this is mine.

ACT 3 / POETHIC

Who am I trying to describe? You wouldn't think of her form by thinking of water. But land wouldn't strike you dumb as thinking either. As reaching either, or engulfed mind—you wouldn't think of her form by thinking about how she moves. Leaded slug like limbs thickened like something to hitch meat to swung spun out, no give, let no remorse seal the deal, swing the gate, latch the teet of when you wouldn't think of her form by thinking about thing. No-thing as object, less. Subject owns object, but what if the object cannot be held by hands nor feet.

[l o n g   p a u s e]

The loop. No-thing. Catgut.
Catgut. A no-thing.

[p a u s e]

In that public place that is opera, man is not submitted to any constraint - he goes there for his own pleasure.
Opera only promises the man what it gives in that moment, there and then.

Theatre is the formal expression of the world
Opera is the informal expression of the world

In text I come to you like a dog. The you is me here please don't flatter yourself. Ears clipped I hear it all including the pitiless yells from the floor below.

The figures stand. And sit down to stand to sit down. Click clack to sit down. Here there to stand, to sit down. Here here and hehes in a game of whack a mole; they bob up as we go down.

[p a u s e]

An operatic shift,

[p a u s e]

because operatic bob sounds too waterlogged. An operatic chorus of voices
yelled in excelsis yelled in exchambers. The choir master makes sure the operations are in order in order, to stay in order.
Up and down a mole gets whacked in demand for order
he/she for their demands. This is all to describe how the houses of parliament thrive on the opera when question is time.
With all gesticulation, no pointed arrow. All whack a mole, no change of the guard.
All game, no shame.

No you can't ride with me but you still catch the bus for free: you'll be alright sweet baby. You okay sweet baby? Don't forget the corner's sweet baby, no, the other side sweet baby. Don't stop sweet baby, keep it up keep your head up, sweet baby. It's necessary to have put one's hand in one's own sex: cut Hand, dead Sex.

And who are you? Why do you. I feed this voice. Who the fuck am I? Why don't I have all the answers for you when you ask. I want to care but I don't know. I need a hand or to see it from someone else.
I'm not an innovator; I'm trickster.
What is that disjointed trickster unbalanced - neglected?
Subjectivity occasioned by action born of breath.

60s music brings me back to good times when I wasn't alive. These times aren't good times
they are eclipsed by virtue signalling in the place of–
good art eats you up to spit you out and toi toi toi.
Go in peace to love and serve the Lord.
But not caged in western time, the line is my friend, remember
finger follows the lined, we can walk or pause at self will. As time it doesn't get
to float. Time is a grandfather; a rooted figure. Always to be spoken of as construct
but once written-stamped-embossed, the bent lines of intention to fact checked
become time.

[l o n g   p a u s e]

Time: opening possibilities for defining black performance as process rather than product.
Time: for arrival, no more for landing

[l o n g e s t   p a u s e]

Please make your exit at the end of the next loop.

[END]

JESSICA LYNNE

A *FORTH*COMING, AN ENDING, AN *ACCOMP*ANIMENT

ESSAY

I have been asked to present an accompaniment. Perhaps a text that might speak to or in concert with the 'I' of *Catgut* as it performs across three acts. This 'I' has levelled at its audience a series of provocations which unfurl in a chorus of 'you' and 'we' and 'us'.

I am telling you this because I am concerned with my placement within this chorus. That is, the 'you' and 'we' and 'us' of this audience are not all the same. There are white folks watching and listening. There are non-Black folks of colour witnessing here as well. And, of course, I am also among my people; other Black folks in the audience. Black performance necessitates this delineation. Who looks? Who looks away? But you (ah, my own chorus begins to emerge) know this already so perhaps I can be direct: you. As in. I am talking to *you*, Black folks.

I'll riff from Margo Jefferson on this one. The beginnings of my own enunciation is informed by the critic's most recent memoir, 'Constructing A Nervous System'. In recounting an origin source for her teen self's 'performative energy', Jefferson details the 'rhythm, the pace, the structure' that defined the heterosexual dancefloor courtships of her youth. The second person announces this memory for Jefferson, giving her the "adult feminist satisfaction" of not being alone in 'those teen girl feelings'.

So too, will I choose the plural 'you' as I attempt to talk about this act of companionship. I want the satisfaction of knowing that this is an in-group conversation. Even if you personally disagree by the end of it all. In doing so, this black writer ventures toward a response to the performer's call, which would have me begin with a confession.

I don't know much about the mechanics of opera as a formal artistic expression (I know the names of our firsts and our brightest and so on…) and you can make your judgments about that. I'll accept them. But I do know what it means to attempt creation against and in opposition to. Me, a black writer coming live at you directly from the centre of a rotten empire. So, in ACT 1, when the 'I' declares that *Catgut* is an opera in

opposition to something
The something being the consistently growing worldwide alt right government and capitalocene.

I know that what is happening is an attempt to breathe anew as the flames consume the very thing that's been choking us. I know that this is an opera chasing after new horizons of form and language, which is to say that it belies my traditional understanding of the aesthetic itself. This is no easy task as Thulani Davis reminds us. I'm thinking here of the truths she writes in her poem 'For Ishmael Houston-Jones':

Working in new / forms, stepping / outside tradition is / like taking a solo…

The sound becomes / a shape, a dance, a / configuration of what / we know that we have / not seen or heard that / way…

Indeed, a fire burns. For before the 'I' announces its *oppositions*, it names its *desires*. A moment in the overture worth lingering on:

I rest scorched and seek intemperate fires

Intemperance signifies the lack of restraint and moderation. It implies a kind of insatiability, an inability to be quenched or contained. Throughout the overture, our author responds to Ben Jonson, indeed Queen Anne herself, with what I perceive to be a fervour ablaze. And though this overture will never reappear before us, I still wonder where the fire goes. What if I am meant, in accompaniment, to follow after its embers here on the page? Though this question is also a serious one for my actual Black life. What fires do I ignite, follow?

The *opposition* is, for me, that which is consumed by the fire and I wonder if our librettist dares us to follow them through to the other side. This, I submit to you then, is the one such consequence of the operatic as presented in *Catgut*. How do you write for a world to come? I don't want to be dampened by complacency. I desire my writing, my questioning, the very matter of my Black life, to evade a cooling. This is to say that I want to be always in the making of an otherwise.

And so, let us return to ACT 1 where our librettist also articulates this question in a more exacting manner:

How do you write for performance the questions in the air?

These are my questions in the air:

Are we prepared to give ourselves over to the unknowns of a future which we are making for ourselves?

How do you write for a forthcoming?

How do you write for the end of the world?

With a form that steps outside of itself. With the embers of a future tense. With an unruliness of a present. With a new dance.

I write this to you with the full knowledge that Black cultural creativity is appropriated for and to capital, as Rinaldo Walcott asserts, while the Black life-form who is its author can be killed for the same creativity. I'm saying this as I think about what then is at stake for the Black performer. For the 'I' performing across three acts as embodied by both librettist and her three orators. For a black writer now arranging her notes in response. We cannot allow ourselves to be swallowed by empire. We cannot allow ourselves to be decimated by these institutions so clamouring for our presence in their own thin attempt at 'reconciliation'. I think about this as I watch the orators take their place inside the Serpentine Pavilion on a cool September evening. Can our utterances within such contexts actually yield the fire? You see, there are no easy answers. I remain in contemplation.

To this end, I've been contending with fahima ife's theorising on movement, fugitivity, and Black life because maybe what I am trying to articulate is not, in fact, the *choreography* of it all, but instead, the *anachoreography* of it all which ife outlines as "the recursive practice of refusal vis-a-vis the choreographed apparatus of coloniality, its methodologies, its origin stories, its naming rituals, and its movements". The 'I' of *Catgut* continues in ACT 1:

Who can reframe Black performance without creating more pain from its reperformed enactment?

With ife in mind, I ask in response: can Black performance ever refuse a public spectatorship which imposes upon it the vicious matters of coloniality? What and where are the covers?

You see, writing this accompaniment is an exercise in learning, which in turn is an exercise in vulnerability because what if I trip up?

Below, ife writes further of anachoreography:

> ...i wanted an anachoreographic opening, a way of moving out and beyond and into not a mimicked dance, an errant movement, not moved because some external apparatus has willed the body to move (through punishment, through force), but a progression of undulations (through trance, through transcendence). And, here, i mean movement/dance, quite literally in terms of how a body moves (alone, together, beside the apparatuses of coloniality), and also hauntologically in terms of what porous anteriority moves through a body, what worlds a body gains (is opened to) in movement.

What I am attempting to reach is the place of the ungovernable position, the site of refusal to capitulate to the disciplined order and expectation of violence. I believe the opening, as ife remarks, lives there. This thought is sweet to me, dear reader. That we might be moved by forces of our own pleasures and desires and not the result of violences as in survival mechanisms. Here, I contend that when the 'I' proposes the *long journey to the edge of your mind to annihilate a fear*, an anachoreographic opening might live in that gesture.

And what if you then say: Dear black writer, you have missed the mark.

I suppose then I would have to allow myself a moment of revision.

But if *catgut is no-thing, the loop, the no-thing*, which certainly traps *them* – those watchers and witnesses that night at the Serpentine, those reading my thoughts this very moment – it might also be the site from which *we* are imagining the befores and afters and beyonds of our bodies:

alive outside the line off the line
tangential to the name
outside time

I kept trying *to make of opera a pure and simple convention as one only gives to numbers a digit value.* [*What*] *a remarkable mistake.* Yes, then. Convention be damned. Convention will always find its ending. This is an opera unsettled and unmoored.

Because what this really is, is a form for an undoing. Consider what the librettist says in ACT 2:

It feels like everything ends with fire. But what if the flame was where we begun.

Of course, the late Aime Cesaire might answer this way, returning the interrogative:

"What can I do? One must begin somewhere. Begin what? The only thing in the world worth beginning: The End of the World, of course."

What if we began with the very thing which frightens them? Me, a black writer declaring that "we will (and choose to spend) our time before death living not passing our time until death dying". Rosamond King has told me this and so I am passing the message along.

Thus, if we are to start at the end of the world, the flame – and I do find this a sweet beginning – shouldn't we determine the how of it all? I wonder if the act of burning can be a performance, too. The anachoreography of it all. And since we are talking about beginnings and endings, this is a moment for this black writer to assert her belief in the incongruence of time. It's nothing linear, especially for us (am I telling you things you already know?), so if we are beginning at an ending in order to destabilise some shit, to reorganise our cosmos then yes, unruliness is required.

In this, I learn too from Dr. Katherine McKittrick who questions the methodology for studying the violent apparatuses that surround us. Can unruliness also be a disruption to the expectations we have of and the logics that order the Black body as it performs? Even those expectations that are named (however righteously so) by us? In '(Zong) Bad Made Measure', McKittrick worries the biocentric order which has so long positioned the 'black body' as a particular type of analytic. What else is possible when the study of black life, black resistance, emanates from a place that does not begin with harm? Can we refuse the black body as a mere theoretical conceit and object? She writes:

> How is the black body, in itself and by itself, tasked with illuminating inequities? Are stories of black resistance only legible in relation to the body that bears racist violence and symbolises preventable black death?

and then again:

> We must ask ourselves – and I ask myself this often – how black bodies rather than black people are informing how we (I) understand liberation and the production of knowledge and, as well, how scholarly work may unintentionally replicate a biocentric order by leaning heavily on corporeal representation.

Self preservation is what's really going on today.

And I do love the way Ms. Staton sings to us: get free, young heart. *Self preservation*. By which I mean, let us transgress black folks. I'm calling the names of some of my kin: Joel, Julia, Nobiana, Reese, Renee, Taylor, Amarie, Camille, Rianna, DeLana, Ope, Assata, Kamau, Najee, Utak, Emmanuel.

Which brings me back to time.

A moment from ACT 3:

Time: opening possibilities for defining black performance as process rather than product.
Time: for arrival, no more for landing

Time here being understood as Black time – a very understanding that has never been contained by the white, western psyche. I want our transgressions to live according to Black time, along the 2 and the 4 as needed, pleasurable and sweet. In this plane, our movements enact new praisesongs that honour our ceaseless becomings. We have been here, between the noise of the planet and the voices of our ancestors as Sister Sonia Sanchez tells us again and again, and yet what if the very function of the opera is to utter that this landing must be shifted? Where is the new ground on which we will dance and shout and love and linger in the profundity of our Black aliveness. Where do the embers lead?

I am saying this still believing that it is us who must continuously call empire's bluff. Every. Single. Time. For what is Black life if not 'constant, unceasing invention in the time of this long emancipation'?

What are we to do otherwise but set the fire ablaze?

Texts that guide this essay include:

Aime Cesaire, *Notebook of a Return to a Native Land*
fahima ife, *Maroon Choreography*
Katherine McKittrick, *Dear Science and Other Stories*
Margo Jefferson, *Constructing A Nervous System*
Rinaldo Walcott, *The Long Emancipation: Moving toward Black Freedom*
Rosamond King, *All the Rage*
Thulani Davis, *Nothing but the Music*

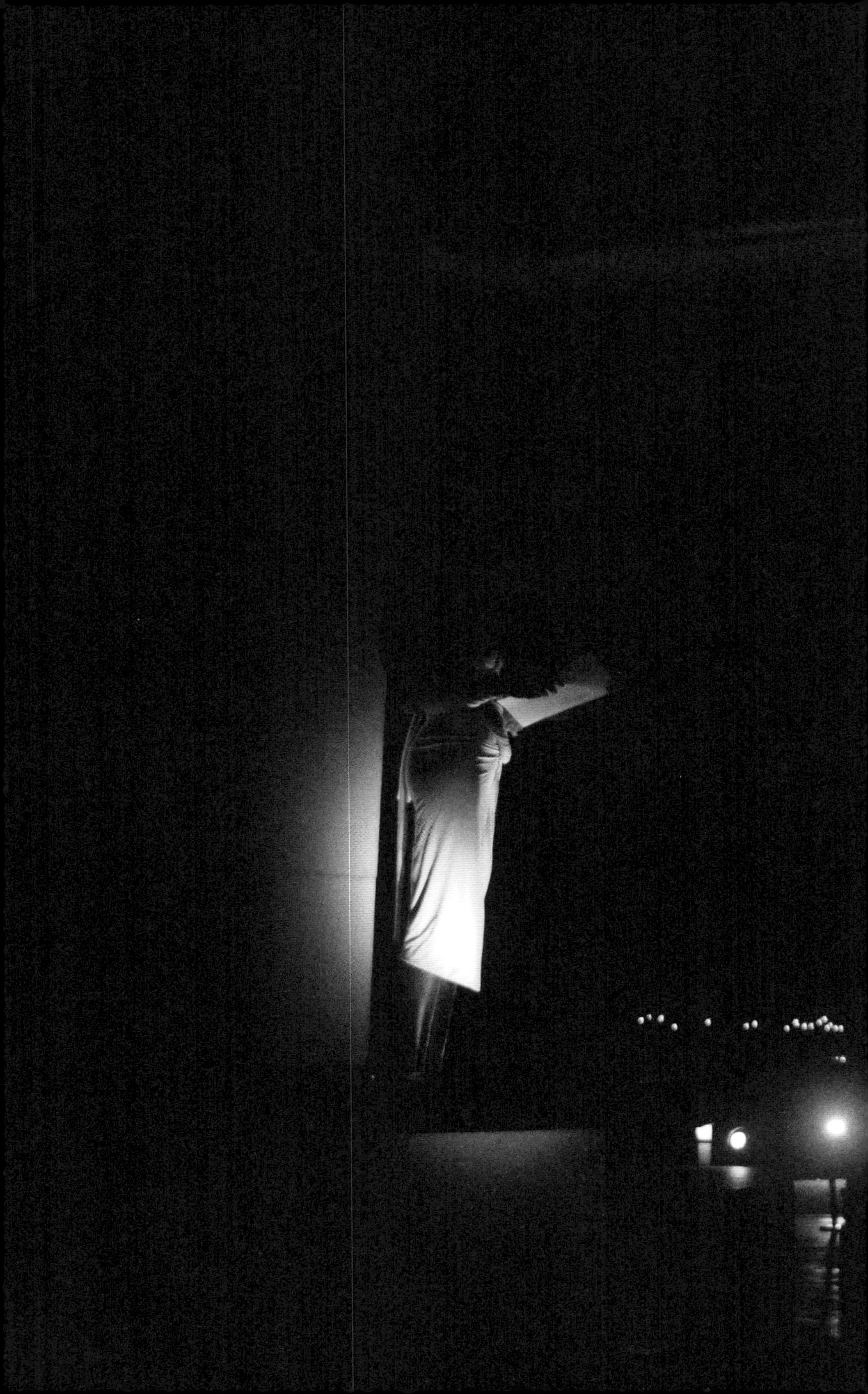

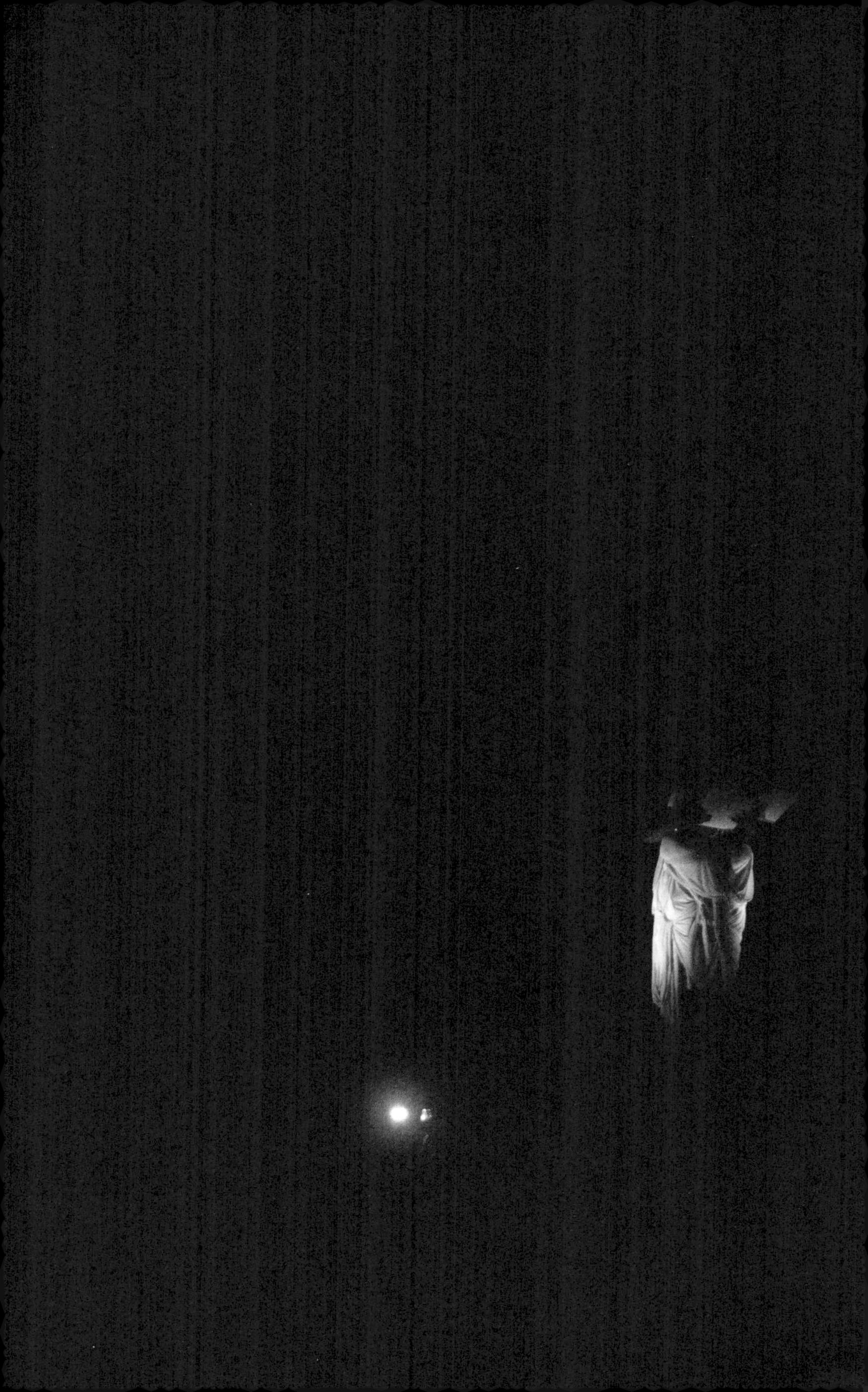

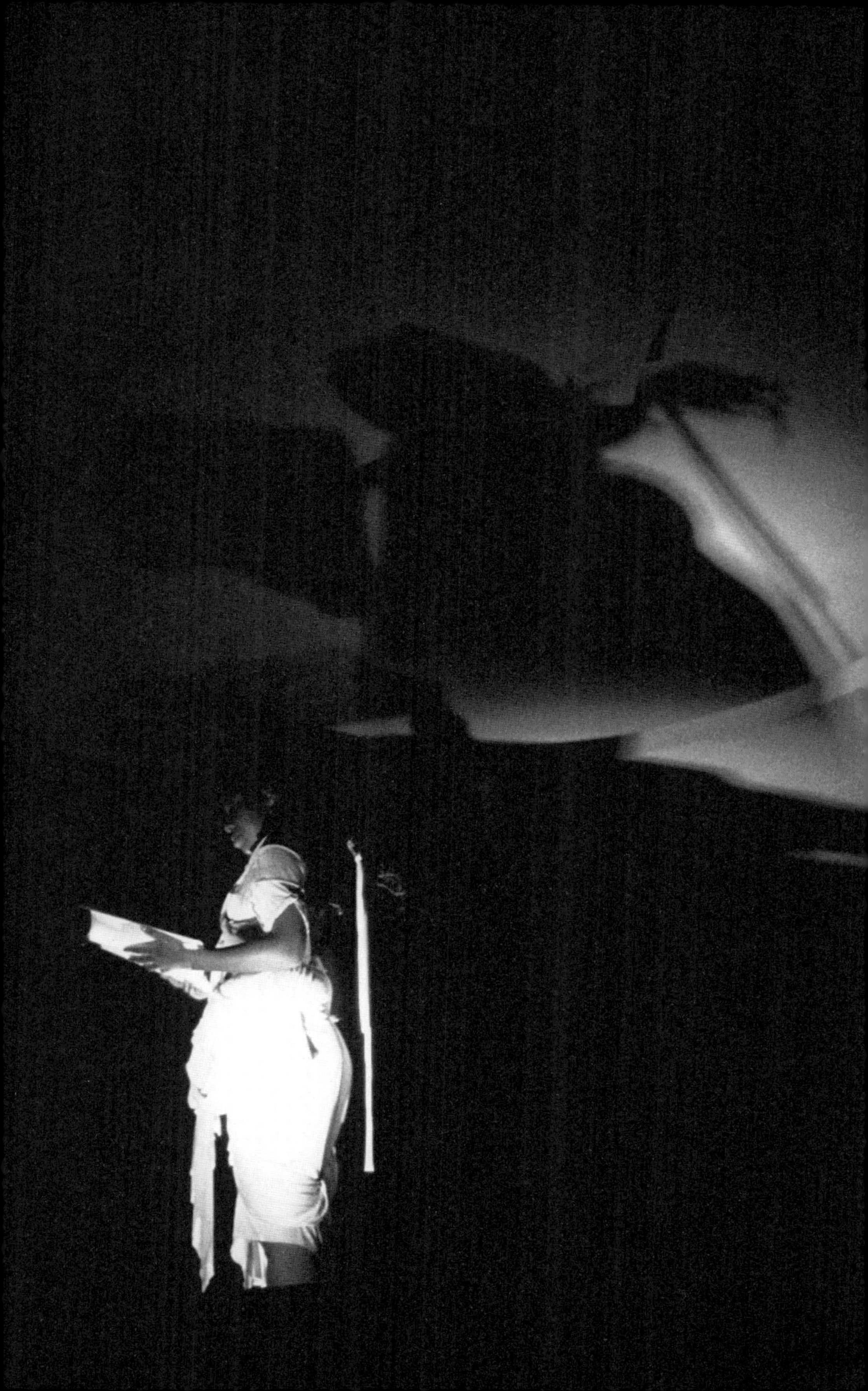

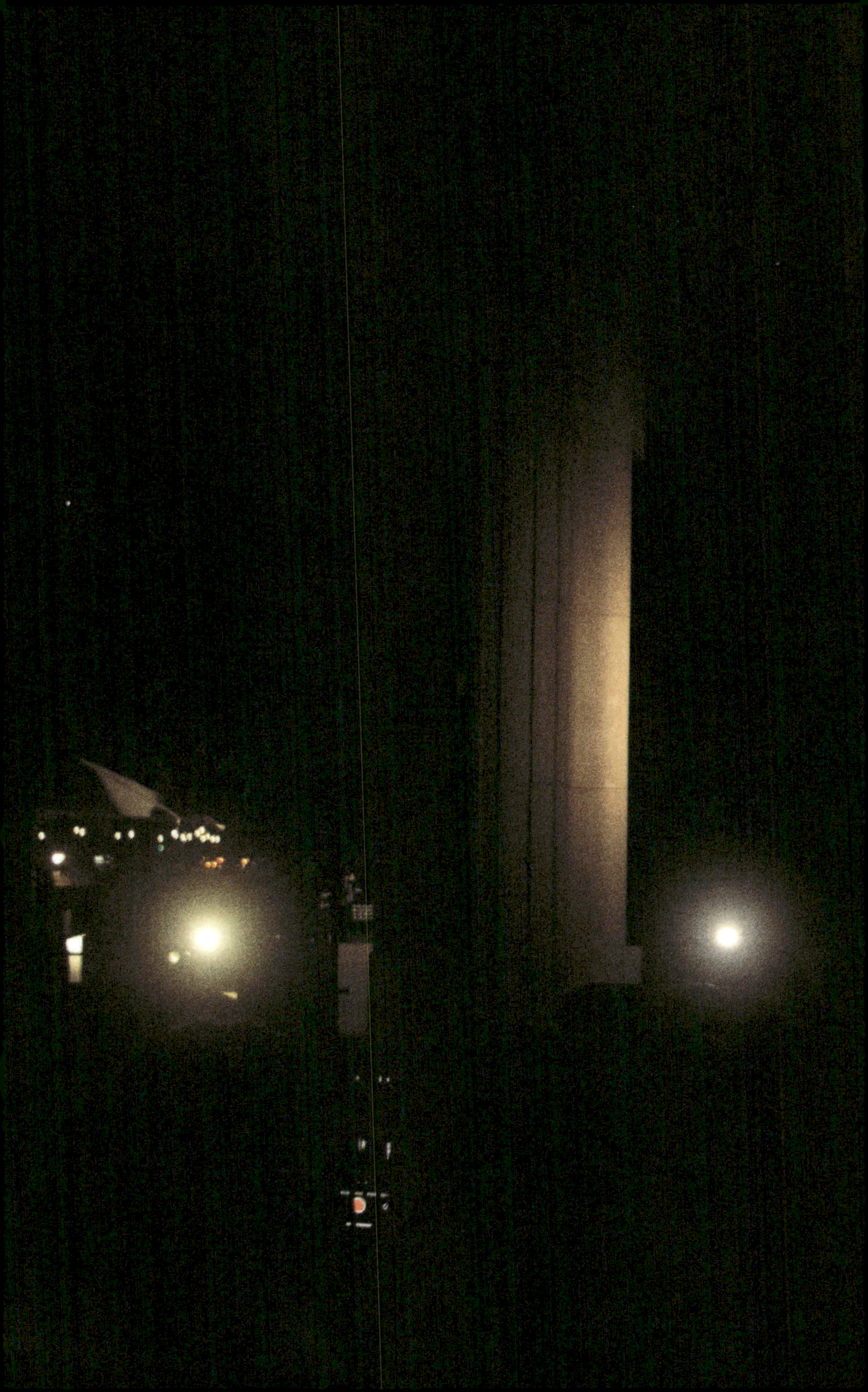

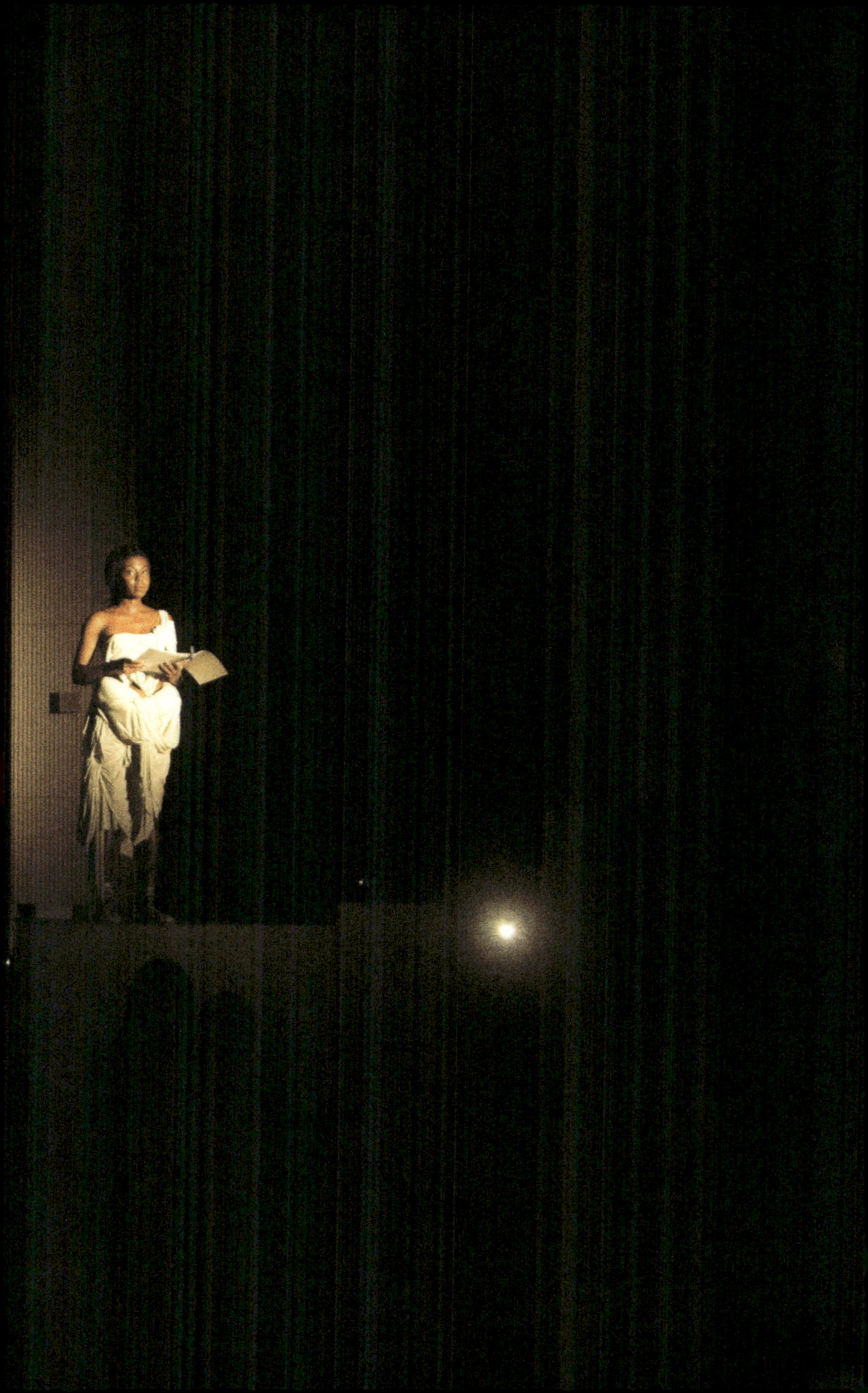

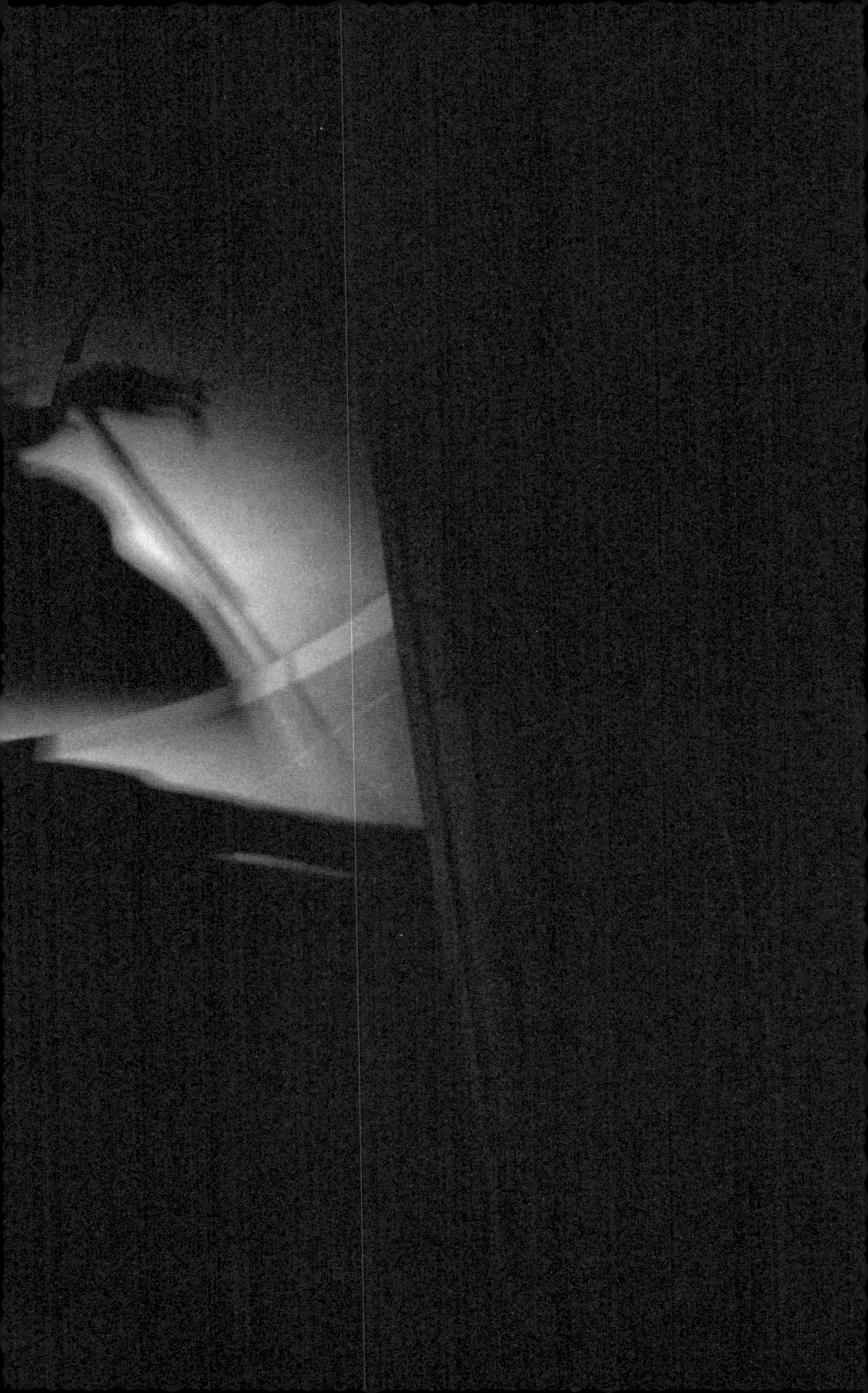

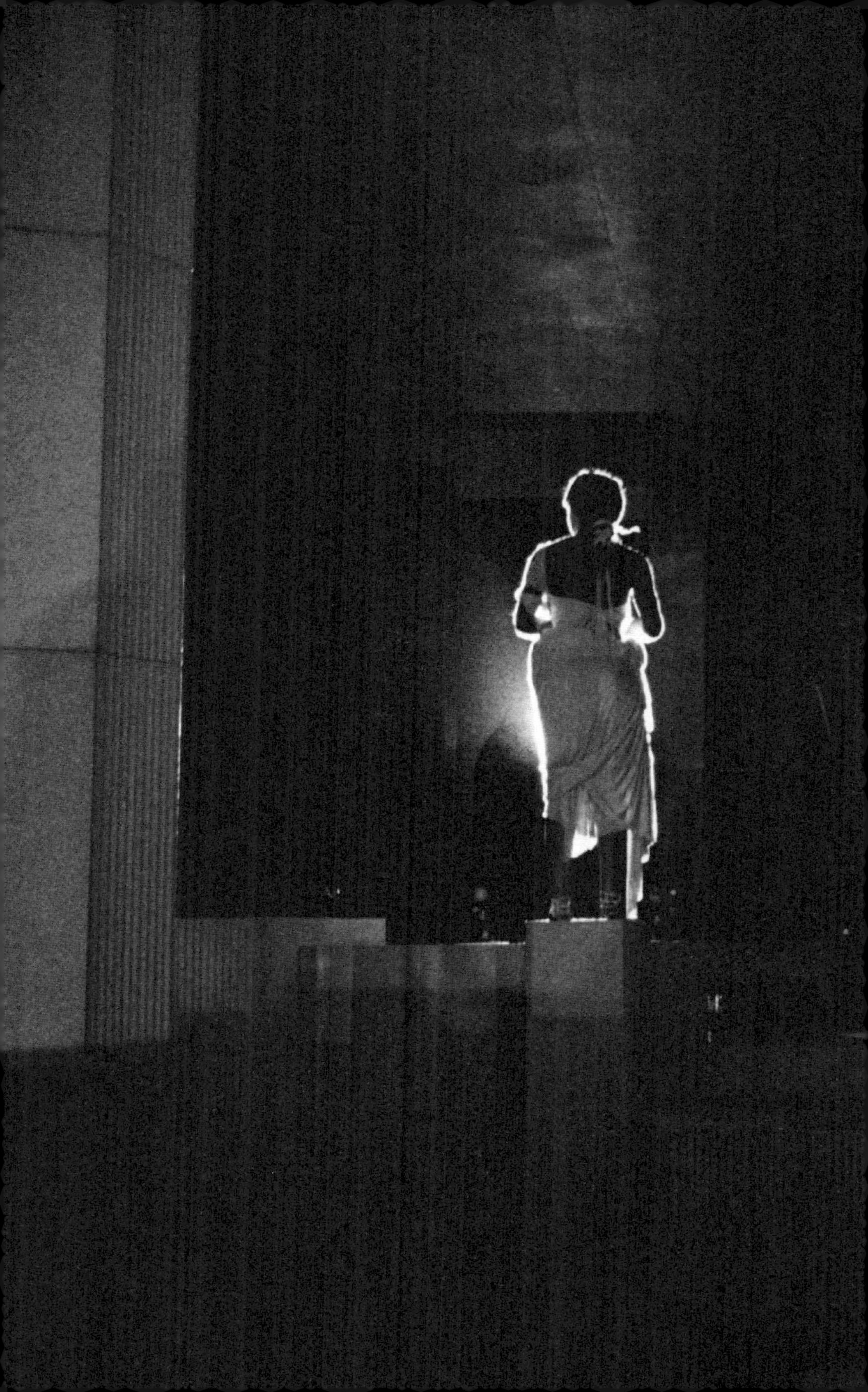

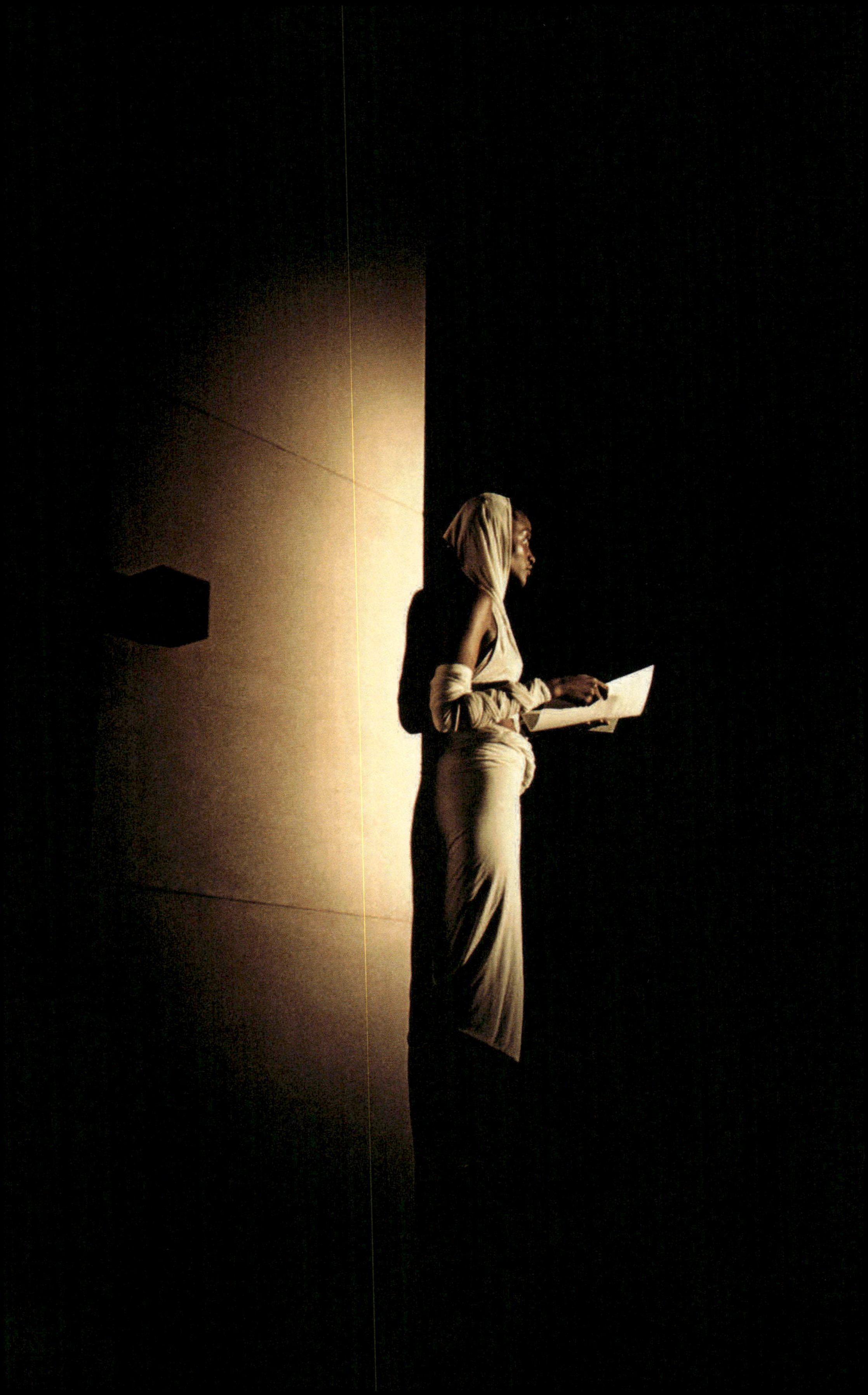

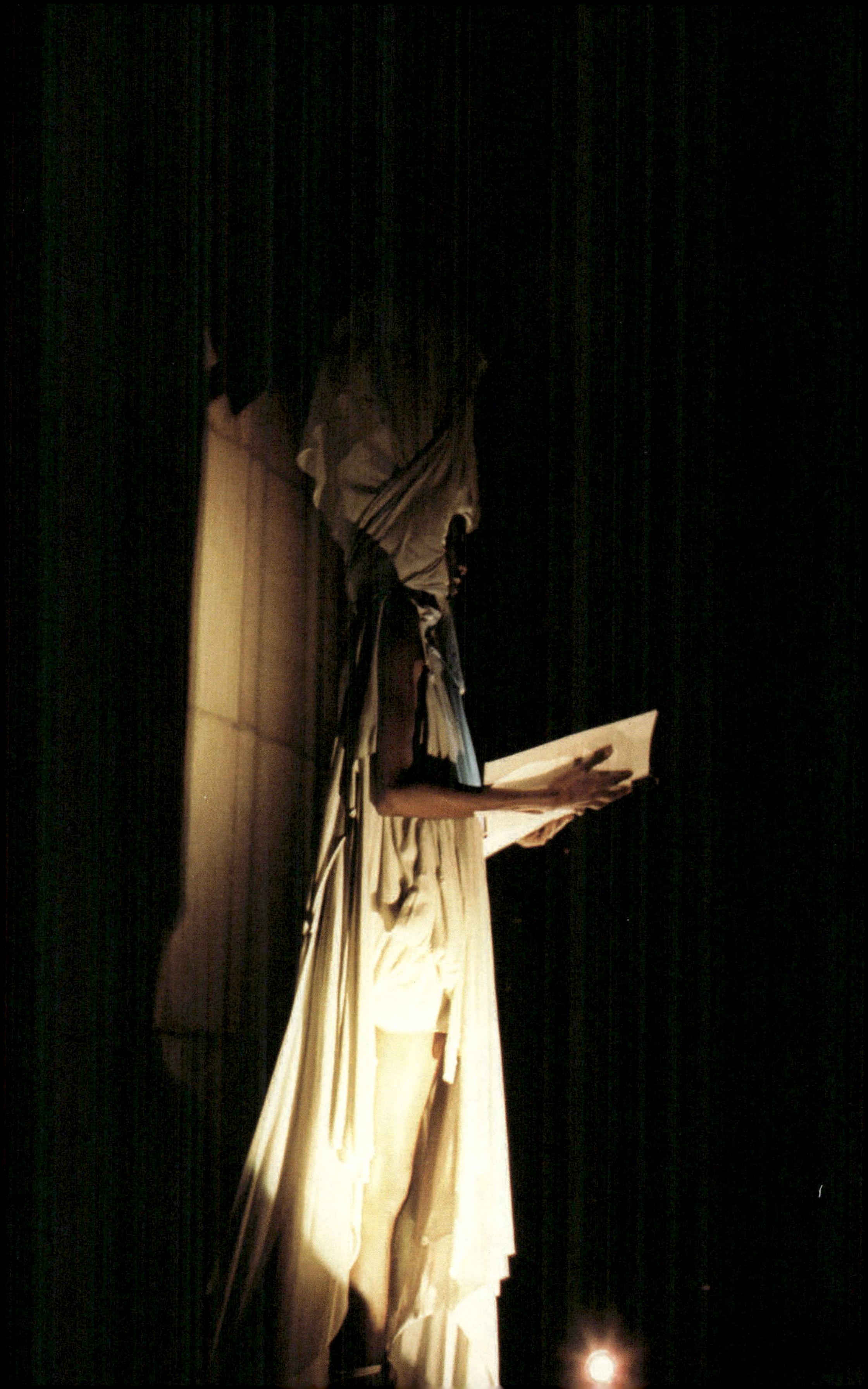

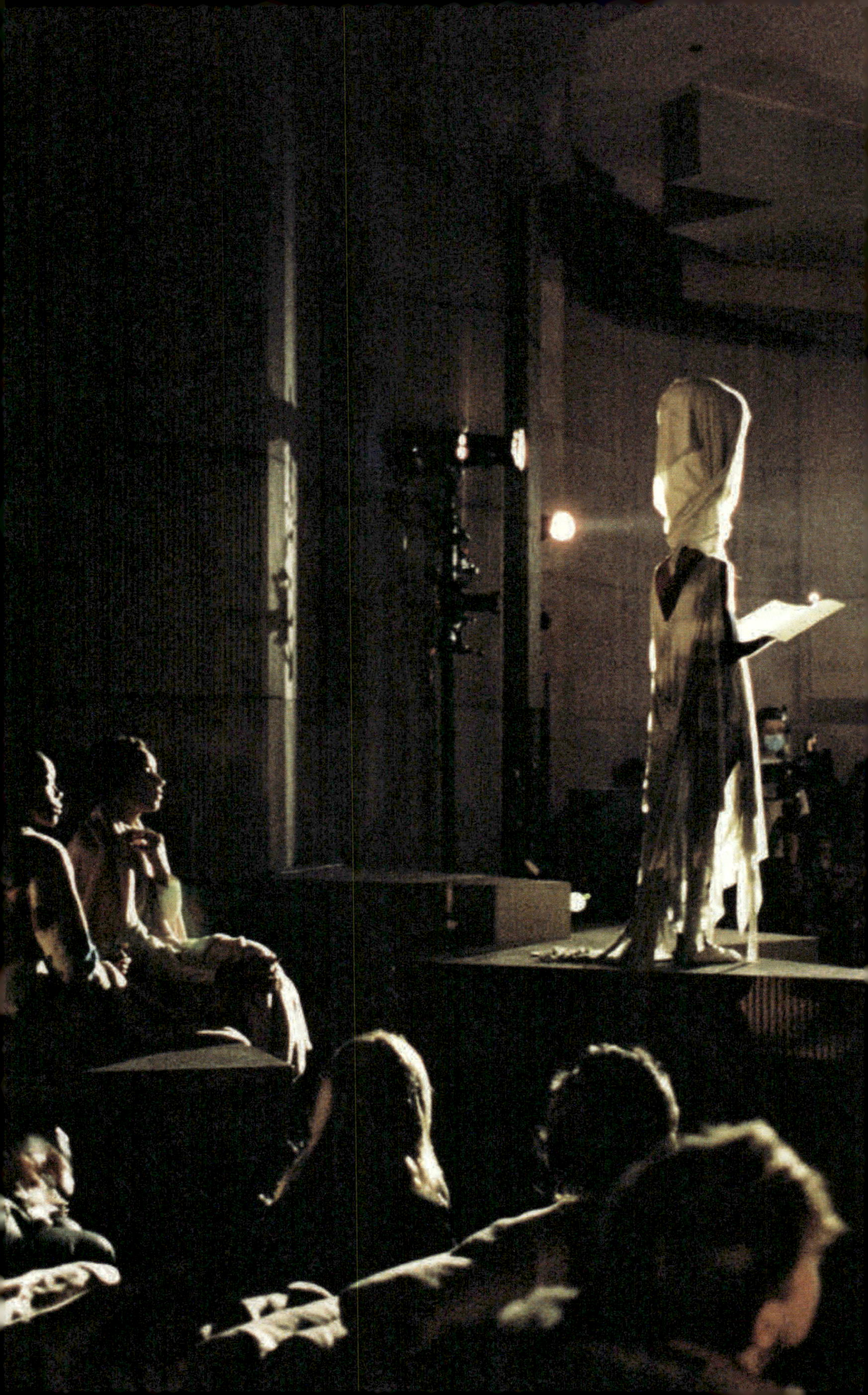

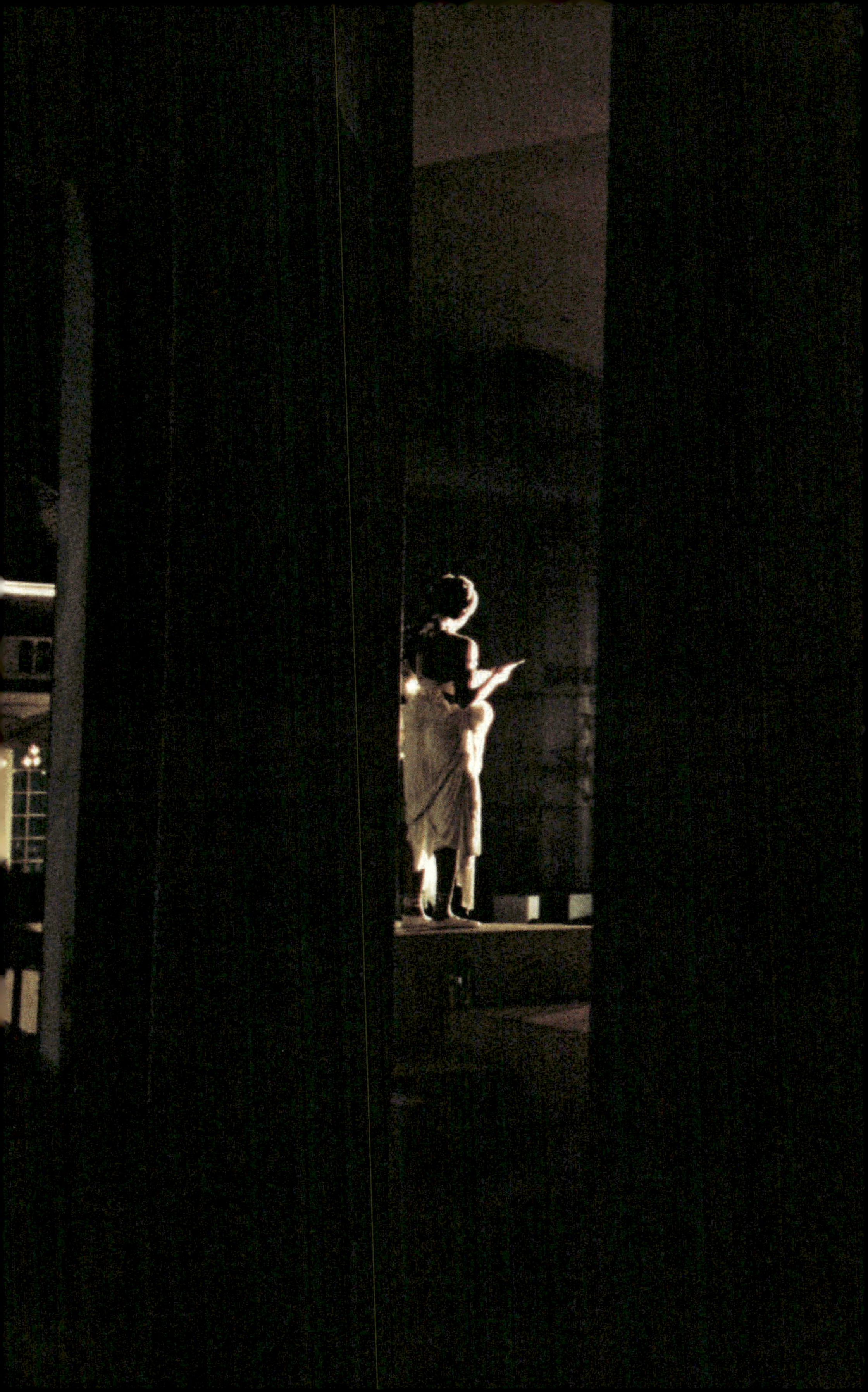

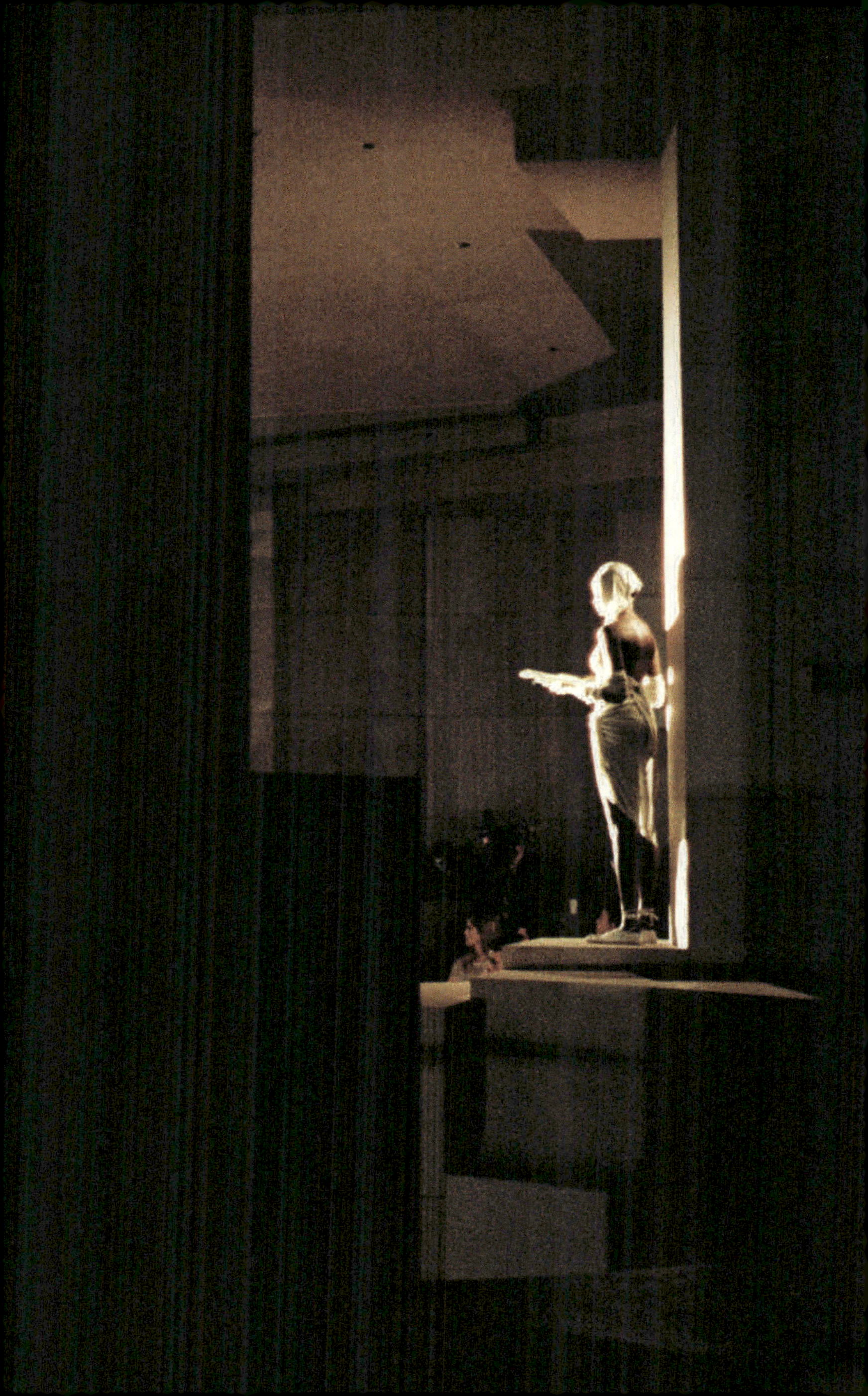

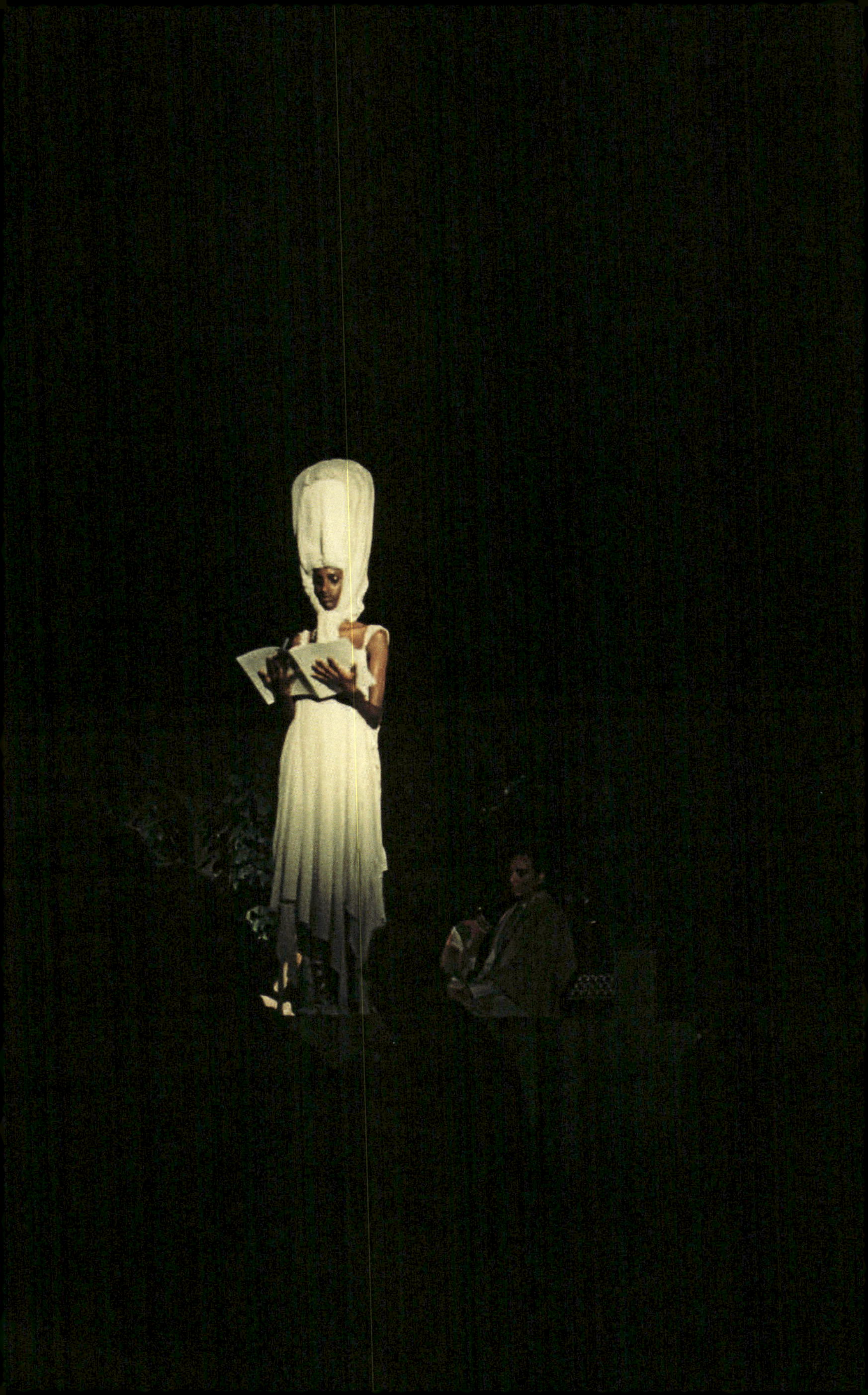

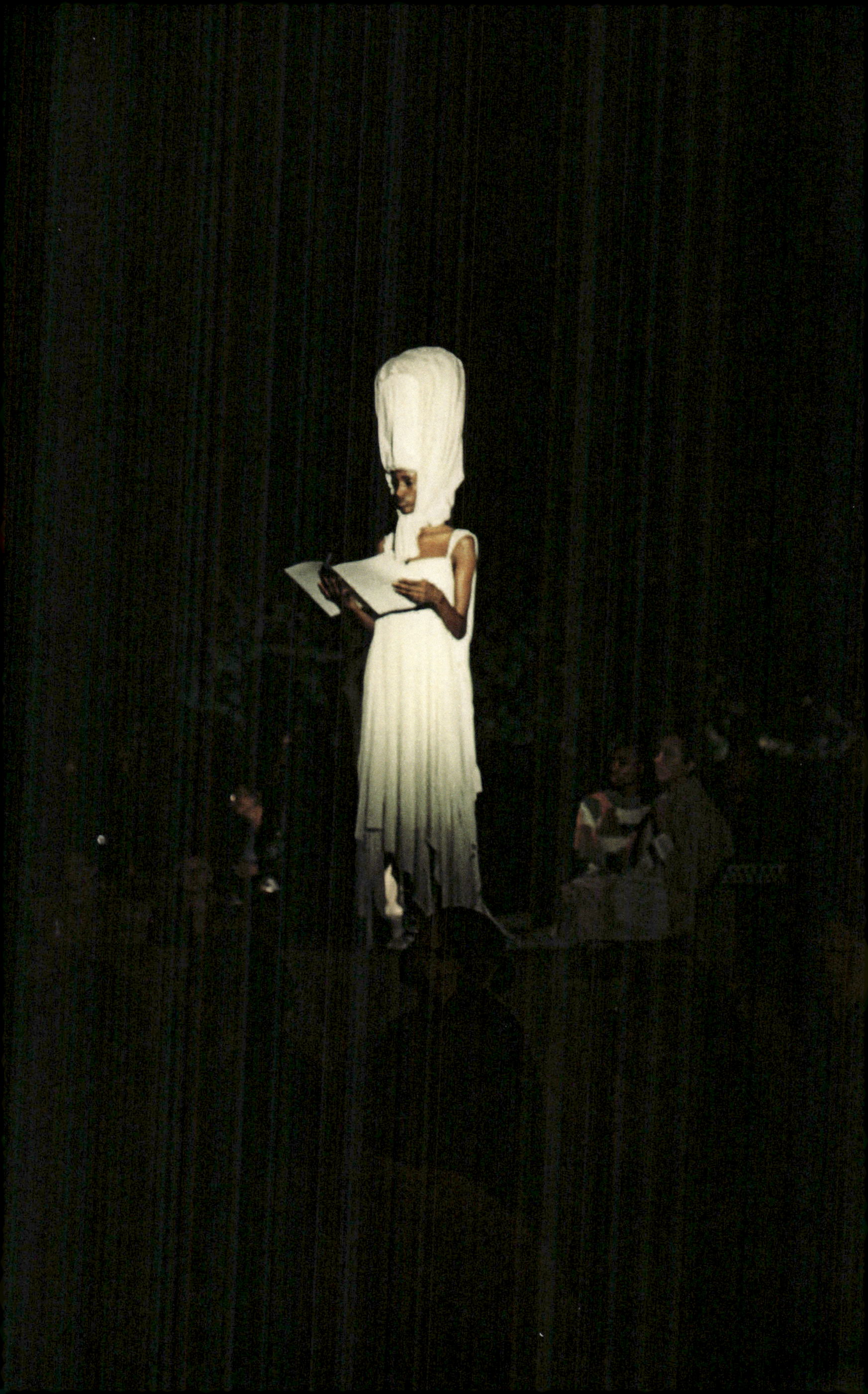

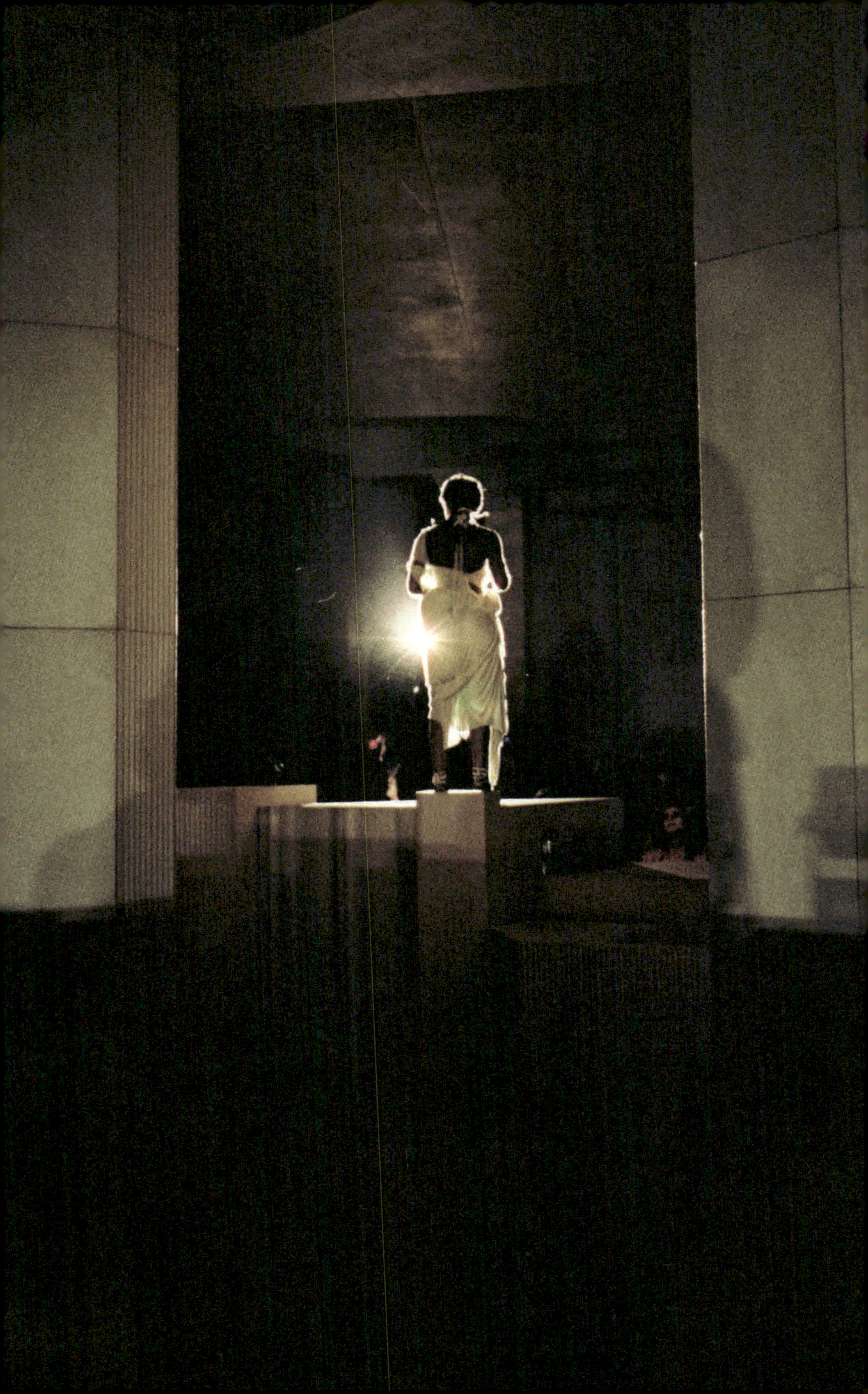

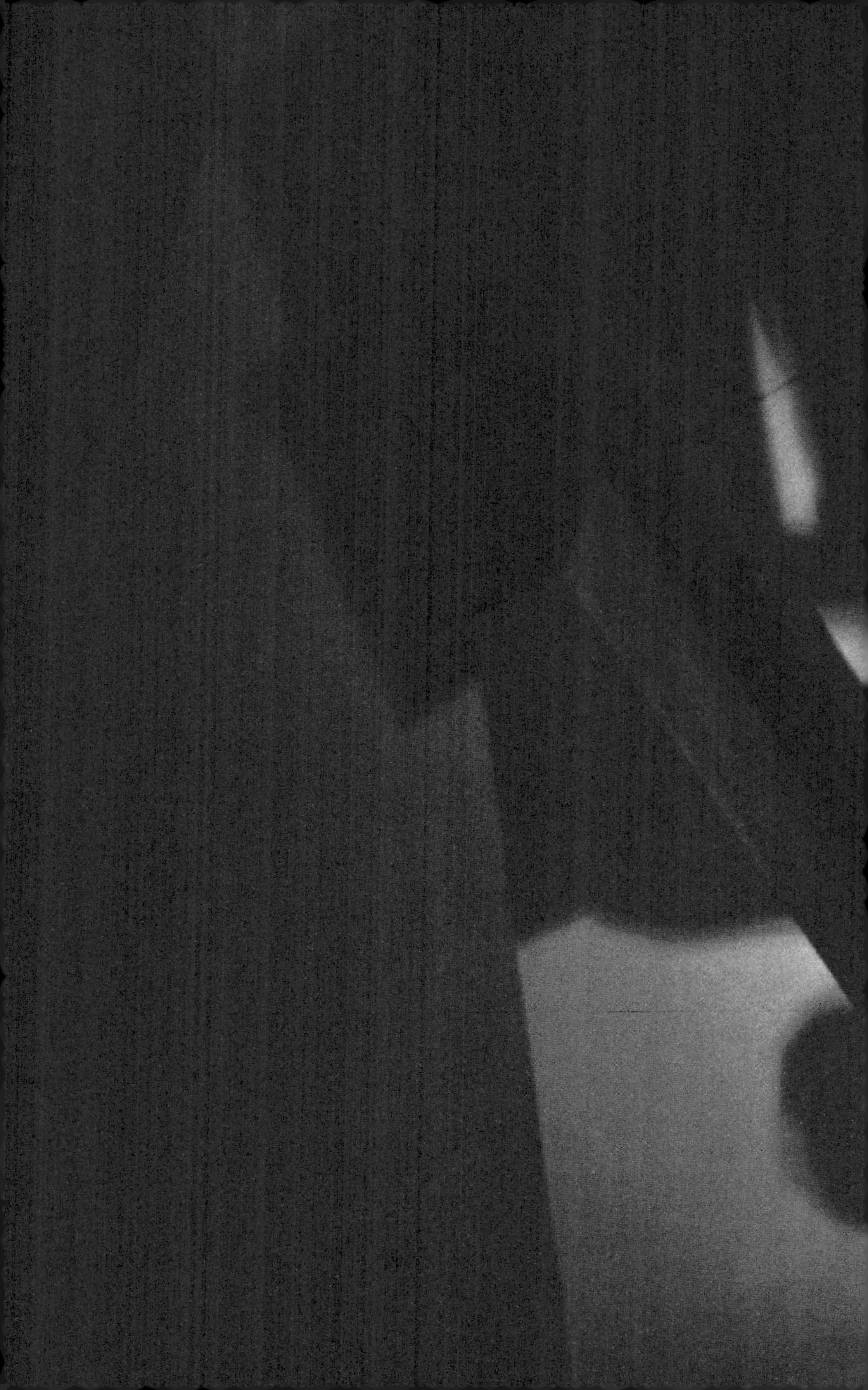

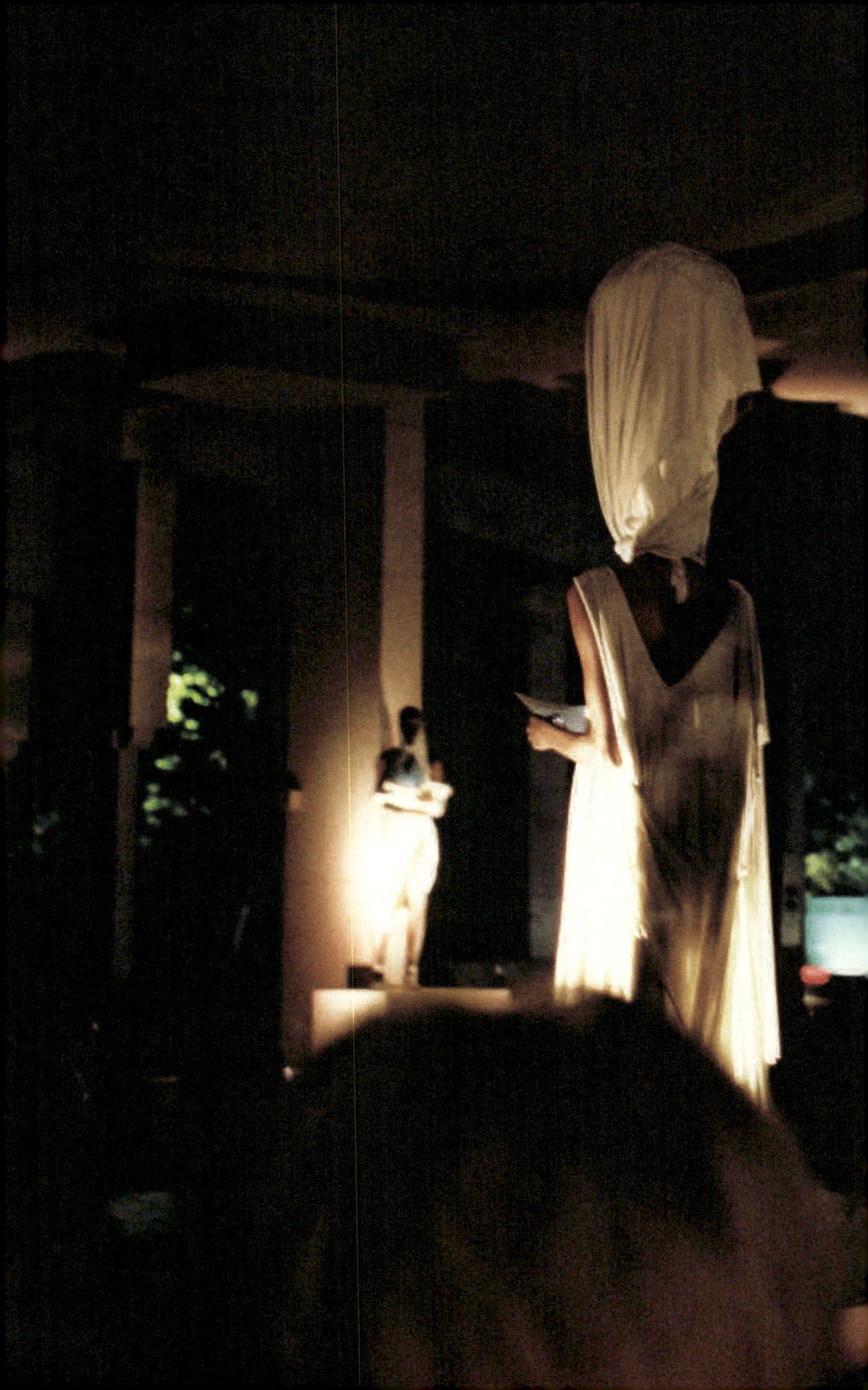

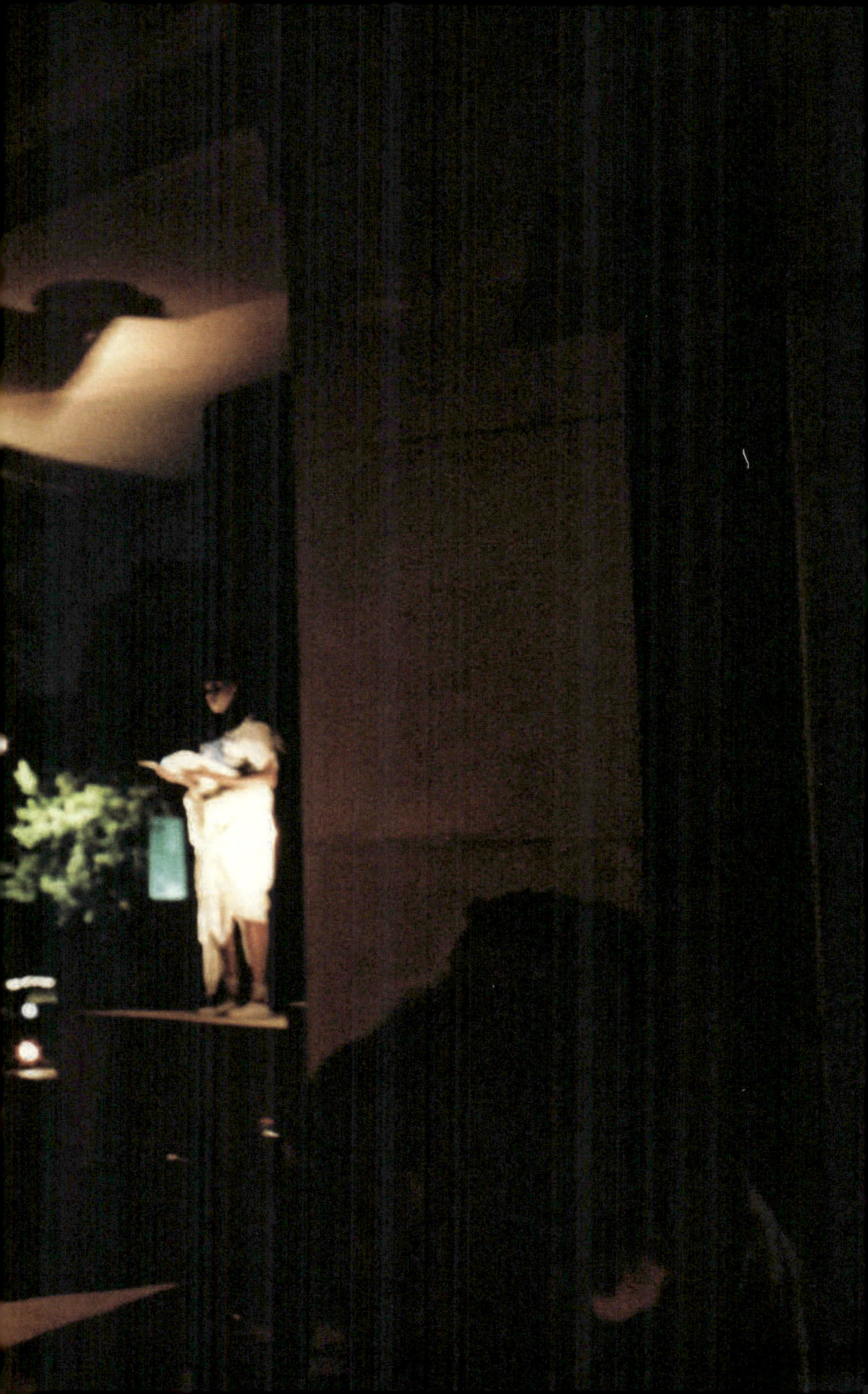

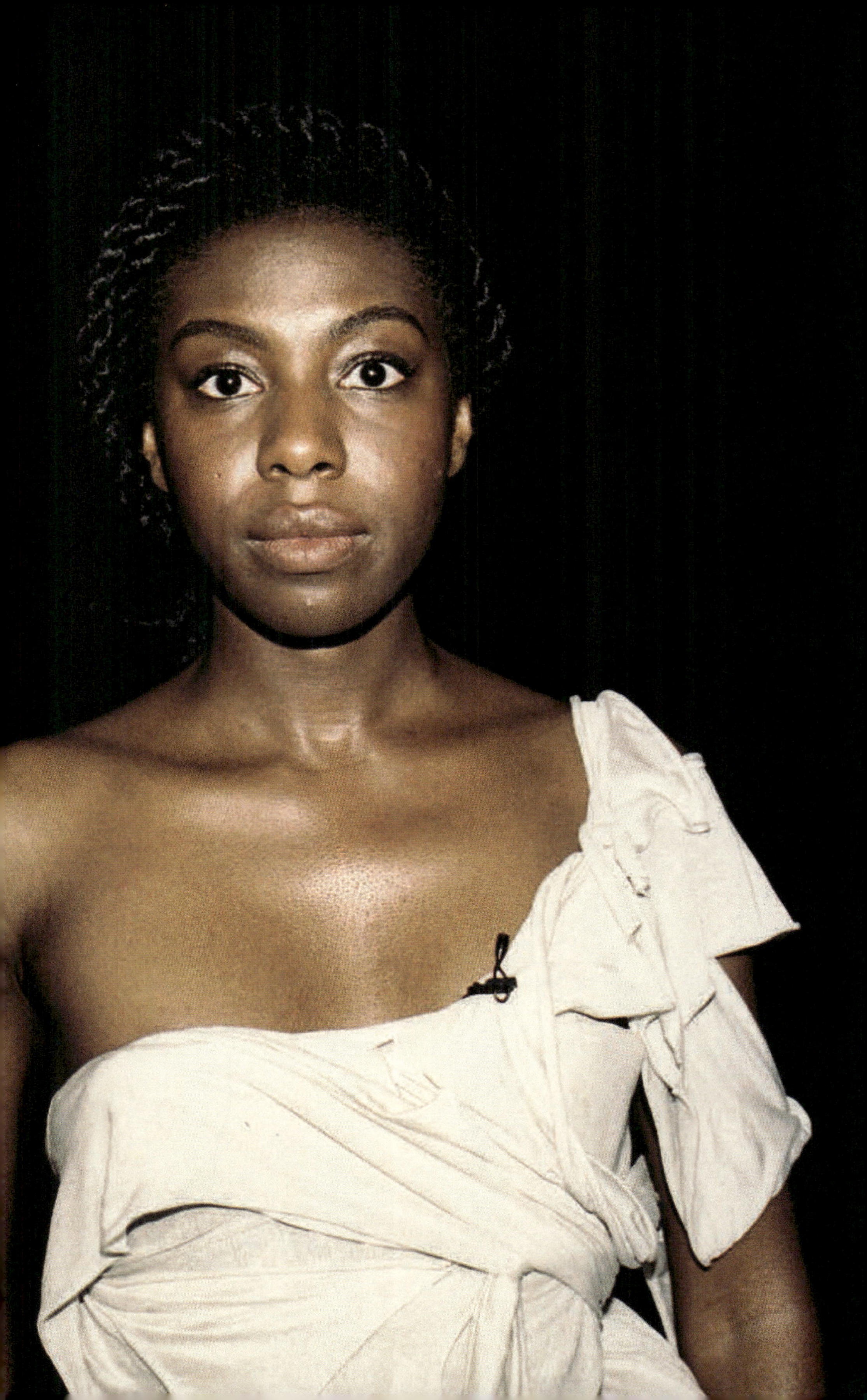

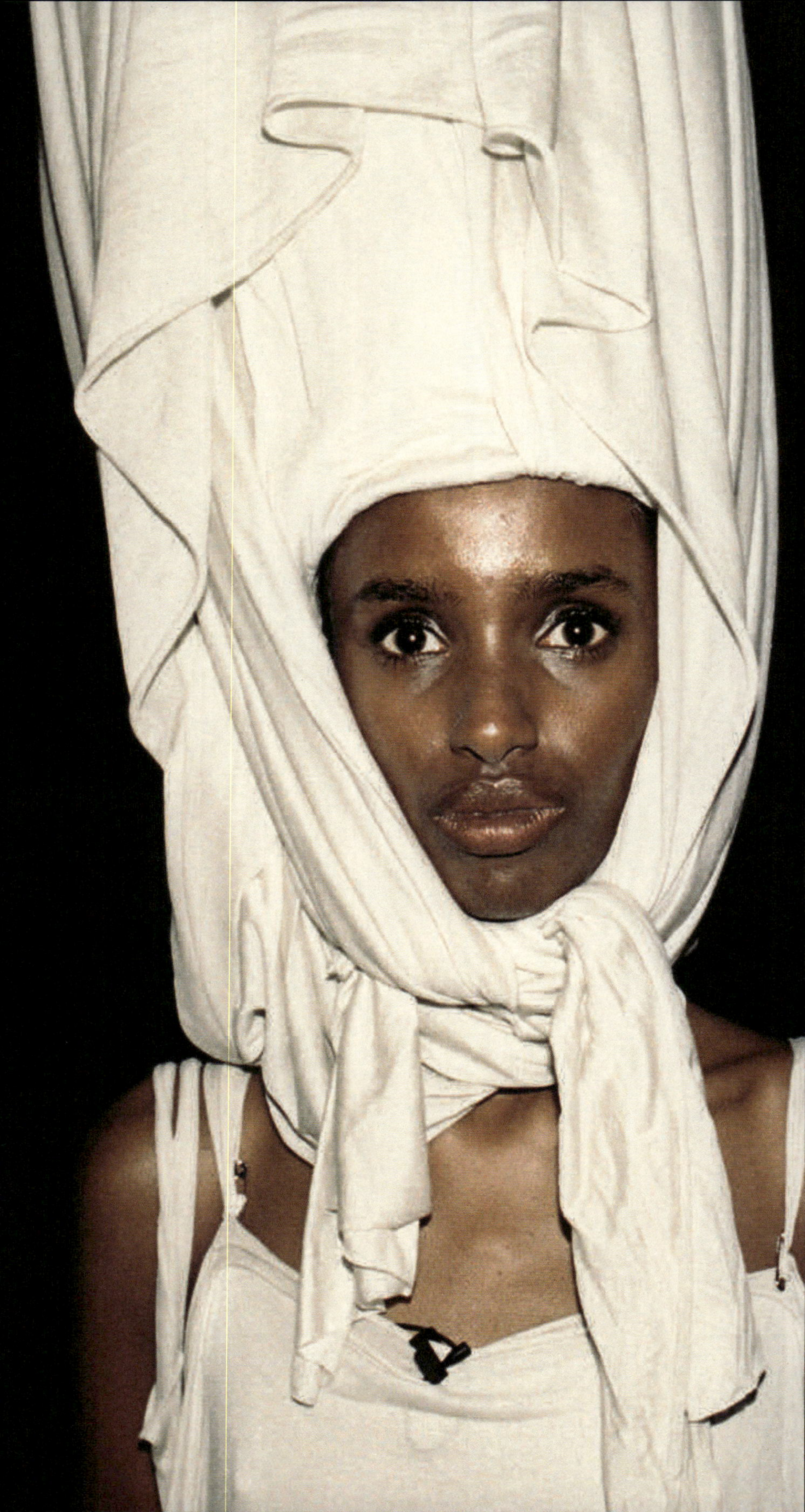

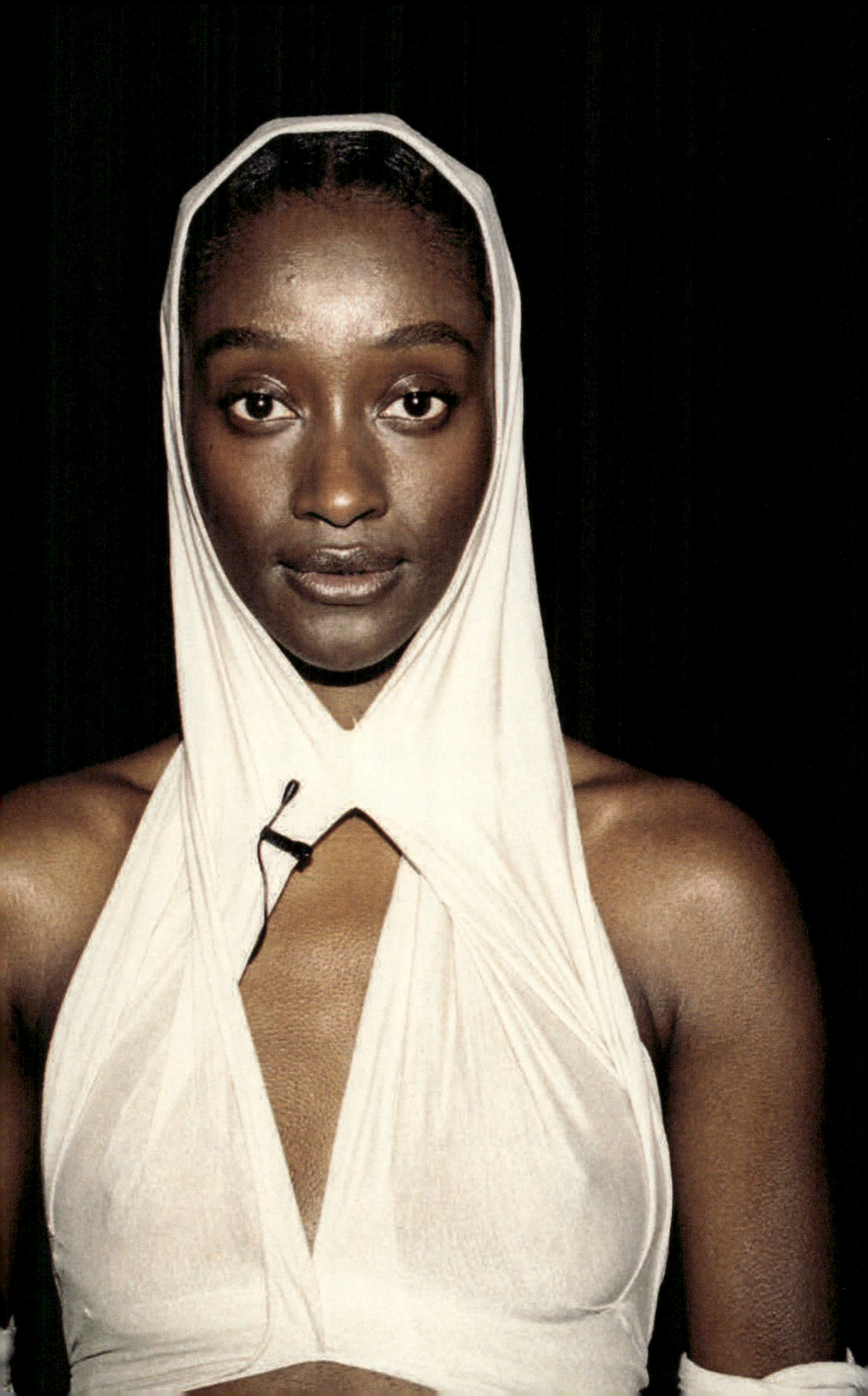

SIMONE WHITE

WE ARE HERE TO SLOW TIME

POEM

[we are here to slow time to break over us not considering so much making poems but where poems come from

“Equilibrations”

create a space that escaped the grasp of power and its laws, without entering into conflict with them yet rendering them inoperative]

come, here, Angel
this is the center of time
time’s backwater
her kerchief her bilge
come here
register
emergency

stand, here, Angel
her dust, her wind
of politics’
vented fire
ventricle left other
cracked
oar
we are in
that see

having been the arch mouth
having been the blank
through which the demon of circles
might
enter

what if
my own being
broken
is the new law

Angel, I am
dust
cover me
velvet   air
blue it is not light
is not invisibilty
it is space
it is visit-
ation

RHEA *DILLON* & ELAINE MITCHENER

IN CONVERSATION*

ELAINE MITCHENER: Opera being a dramatic and musical platform, how do you feel that it was married to *Catgut*?

RHEA DILLON: There's something about performance. It goes back into itself of this ruminating I was doing on the quotidian performance of people and Black people. What is it to perform in your day-to-day? And how does that change? But also how is that never the same in any instance ever again? As much as I have points of perfectionism and ideas for it, I realise that actually the work could never be a version of perfect, text-perfect or libretto-perfect. That was the whole meaning of this term that I was using: a ringdown. *Catgut* was a poetic ringdown dismantling of all of these things and this bubbling pot of ideas, mythologies and criticisms that came to a head at the right temperature. That temperature being the performance.

During production there were these formalities and questions of 'could people hear', 'could people see' (given the pavilion's indoor-outdoor physical structure) that could have been played with and tweaked, but I enjoyed that it wasn't formally an opera. I could be intrigued by further experimentation with the orators if there was more workshop time.

EM: I'm really pleased that you mention 'more workshop time with the orators' because that was something I observed that might have been frustrating for you. It looked great because they looked like statues or like people that came from outer space.

Time is really important. Time on the piece, developing the piece...

RD: But I think what is really interesting about this analysis is following the ringdown formula that I self-set; how long the text is, in reference to the performance and now in reference to the book. There was something I was really intrigued by, in having this point of hyper-narration that could take apart language in a literal sense. That was almost my test and I foresaw the points of feedback where some people would remember 'this line' vs 'another line', because it's so intriguing how even the communal ear breaks off into the individual mind. I'm a hyper-analyst of points of interaction. That's so evident with how *Catgut* comes across, for example. There was a study in the US that found that the average person spends around 3 minutes in a gallery room in a museum. I applied that to an exhibition I recently had at Soft Opening. I have an olfactory work where I wanted the scent to be emitted just under every two minutes so that each person who enters the room could have the fresh experience of it before it morphes and becomes something else, as scents do. I'm really intrigued by the natural confluences of the audience, or frankly 'the public', alongside the direction that a director/artist/whomever is in charge, is desiring to put forward. How do they interact and how have you caused friction?

* This conversation took place on Monday July 18th 2022. It has been edited for clarity.

I was of course aware, and conscious of, the hyperextended narrative weight of the libretto. It raises this idea that the general public has a reading age or observing age of a 10 year old (as is commonly cited in advertising worlds). Whenever that study was taken, what if it had developed to that of a 21 year old in 2021?

EM: This is a really valid point and makes a lot of sense as to why you took that approach. But think of classical Greek orators who used to stand and deliver speeches for long periods of time, it was only until the mid-century as technology has developed...

RD: ...Our post-modern technology invented...

EM: Our attention span has decreased.

RD: Exactly. Societally we keep getting prescribed the notion that we are all going to this place of not being able to tangibly connect with each other. There's another study I found when I was making my final university project film, *The Name I Call Myself*, where it said that the public of today concentrate better with two screens than one. It's almost like this training where the second screen is obviously our attachment to our phones: so many people are on their phones or tablets whilst watching a film, or when framed in the more quotidian, everyone is on their phone whilst walking down the street. I noted that concentration point and said 'okay bet, let me play too'. Let me give you two screens and then you don't need your phone in your hand. It's me you're focused on.

EM: What about bringing a third screen!

RD: I think a third screen would actually push you out. It could push you over the edge into hyperstimulation. That's an interesting conversation too: would that make you not take anything in? This is all to say that thinking about an audience isn't new for me just because this was my first performance. Thinking about the reality of an audience interaction is something that should always be done around any kind of presentation. An exhibition is just another form of presentation and, like performance, is to be received by another. I'm always thinking about playing with or disturbing that synergy whilst consistently being conscious of its hold.

EM: Just looking through your libretto again I was re-acquainted with the way that you repeated certain phrases or words.

This is not an opera this is an omen / This is not an opera this is a sermon / This is not an opera this is a spiritual / This is not an opera this is a room to claim as one's own. No not yours...

Those things are very musical. Musical in the way that they're used as well. Through your research of listening and watching a lot of different types of opera, a sentence can be spun out. 'The cat sat on the mat' could be a three minute aria which takes the voice all over the place so that it's really inventive, but it's essentially still just 'the cat sat on the mat'. Yet your extension gives us a way to listen to that sentence and hook in. Those things for me can be very boring from the opera side of things but when you included elements of that in *Catgut* it inverted it because you brought things that weren't expected, like that ownership of the space:

...No not yours / Becky, Karen, Susan, / Billy, Ken, Graham...

That was so great and funny and that's why I'm so precious about your text and its communication.

How did you find managing your cast and team? This is a thing that people don't talk about. We talk about the big picture. Did you learn about yourself through that process?

RD: I learnt that it was the first performance that I had done yet–

EM: That didn't show by the way!

RD: Thanks. (laughter) It was also a reminder of why I love working in groups. There were these really different personalities. There are different means of getting to the rehearsal room and these different journeys that people are taking just to arrive in the space: some by bus, some longer train journeys, and I found that was also potent in how the orators responded to the text. That's something that can only be listened to through feeling.

Some of the orators had acted before and that was very clear. One of the performers had such a transformation from the auditions to the end. It's really a desire for self-application. If you want it, you do it.

EM: I will say to you that I was very very impressed by the way you handled the orator arriving late to the performance. I could feel so much kindness and understanding. Which I would say isn't always there. Well, I had to learn!

RD: Me too. (laughter)

EM: But I thought you really handled that with so much maturity and as someone who hadn't done that kind of thing before. I thought that was really impressive.

RD: Thank you.

EM: Because she was late she didn't have the sound check where you get used to the space, where you also get to inhabit the space.

RD: So much energy is involved. You're displacing energy in that space but you also need to become one with the energy and the space. When you're asking about what that experience was, and how it comes into play with directing people, in a sense you have to take what they're giving you, as much as what you're giving them. Once they have the libretto in their minds I'm just there to really push them. What I learnt was that it's really important having someone who wants to be there, who wants to deliver what you're saying and is excited by that. I really found that in each of the women. That's the best thing about group collaboration. It goes back to when I was in school and was better at team sports than individual sports because when we could all win together I was so much more excited and thus performed so much better.

EM: I'm the same. I love the collaborative aspect and sharing the energies. I've been really positive that everybody can enjoy it together.

RD: Even if there's a slip-up of an intonation, even if someone fell... if you respond negatively a tension can be created from displaced energy. There's nothing worse than someone who's pissed off on stage. There is no point in you being there. The audience can feel that too.

This also holds true in a sculptural sense. I'll do a site visit before an exhibition because I think it's really important to see the space and also engage in this placement of 'new to the space' energy that you're bringing in, as well as seeing if that existing energy wants to engage with you. It's respect.

EM: Yeah. The waiting of the audience builds this kind of energy and expectation, not tension but an air of expectation because they know something is going to happen. You also had the sound, the music playing before the performance, and that was kind of strange. It was loveable.

RD: I was asking 'what could creating this suspension do?' Playing into the overture space in an opera - what could that be saying about the full work?

EM: I thought that sound suspension was really effective. I don't know how many people in the audience attend opera's or know of its restricted forms. In this incredible space with open sides, you knew how to contain and express the sound you were making in that space. Architecturally it was very engaging, but also the way you moulded that space showed it doesn't have to be someone running about; it's a very subtle thing. People were very focused on what was going on and in fact my space from the exterior was really helpful because I could check the piece out from many different points and different places that it could be viewed from around the pavilion whilst asking, does it still work? That is the thing: does it still work? It's not even for you to answer.

RD: How do you define an opera in its contemporary sense and how would you describe it to someone?

EM: That's the big question isn't it? For me opera is kind of a redundant word now; it's dead. I have a good friend who has a printed t-shirt that reads 'Opera is dead, long live opera'. It's like the 'the queen is dead, long live the king' line that's said when the queen dies. It's very 'that is over, this is reborn,' and I think now is the time where the idea of an opera could be reborn. It's renewing itself each time and it's in the hands of people who are not even coming from traditional classical music routes. Instead, they're coming from very different creative backgrounds and have very different ideas of what a dramatic music event is (dramatico-musico or musico-dramatico; I can't remember the term now). What is the stage now? You could have an opera in the middle of the street. That's the stage now; it is wherever it is. It is where you want to place the action.

RD: That's really powerful to acknowledge because it aligns with the class structure aspect that I was also trying to address and break down. Before I had gone into this period of research I'd been asking, 'if a spiritual is not an opera then what is it?' Questioning what separates spirituals with opera, and how class comes up as the main culprit for this separation. Obviously in the UK I would frame that we have such a point of discussion where class comes first before race.

Having the performance in Hyde Park I was then thinking of Speakers Corner being just across the way and how that was (and still technically is) this direct geographical spot for freedom of expression. The orators being placed on the pillars was meant to mimic Speakers Corner in a minimal way. It's this ability for subtlety to come through that's so important to me, and it meets my sculptural practice. Some people had thought of Speakers Corner and didn't even realise we were in Hyde Park! That was really funny; for people to be so displaced by the work, within a work. And how that can be connected, but also disconnected in this satellite sense.

Now if the performance was going to be somewhere else would the orators be up high or low? And at what point of content would I engage with the politic of the place or/but it is still an opera by a British person? And from and how is it in the UK politic first? Is it really important for me to carry that along? What that should lead to is a question of how citation could be engaged further.

That's a good question to ask you: how do you compose your work around citation?

EM: I tend to use them as the starting point for ideas, so I will see or read something and explain that. That is for me the beginning of other research. Or I look for things that kind of reference that citation but I use it as a springboard to further questions. Often I have a sense of something that I want to share or communicate because it's important to me. Whether it's important to anyone else at that point I don't care: I just need to get it out.

But because I'm not an academic, I'm not a writer, I don't have that gift. Instead, I then have to look and do a lot of reading around things to see if anyone else has thought about the feeling or question I have. Then, I discover that there are other people who have actually expressed what I felt more than what I thought, but in a succinct way. Then I'm like (gasps) and I stop with that. It's really a seed of an idea and then it builds and builds.

I don't know if that's answering your question really because what I've tried to do with my own work is to communicate quite complex ideas and philosophies without diluting them, but communicating them in a way that they can be easier understood, or that people can hear and then reflect. I seem to use a lot of words but actually what I'm doing is sifting through. For example, 'the then + the now = now time' was a phrase that I found, which was based on the philosophical ideas of Walter Benjamin. He was a Jewish German philosopher and thinker who came up with the concept of 'eingedenken' which means: the act of remembrance as an act of responsibility; how we choose to remember things from the past determines and affects our present, and our future. He's looking at historical facts but not being held down by them, instead looking at how we choose to remember them. With the phrase 'the then + the now = now time', which feels very linear, I created this piece using the idea of 'eingedenken' but also joined it with the thinkers, writers or speakers who had similar ideas, like Sojourner Truth or James Baldwin or a quote from the song *Strange Fruit* composed and written by Abel Meeropol (who was a Jewish American communist and considered to be a traitor) and is made famous by Billie Holiday. I didn't know this information and I came across it and thought, 'okay, this has really changed my feelings about the song in itself'. He was referring to something that was very present but that was steeped in past actions of America and what was going on at that time... These citations I use as a way to liberate my mind and open me up to possibilities of expression. Sometimes it has been like a spider's web that I'm caught in and can't move! But you just have to break it, start again and then start spinning in a way that you can find your way around, because one thing will trigger another. That's the exciting thing with a spider's web: something lands on it and triggers something else. That's another idea I have about how to describe what's happening in the world. Stuff that's happening in Ukraine is affecting what's happening in Ethiopia right now, because people are starving as they can't get grain that they usually get from Ukraine. Some could say this is Eastern Europe, what's that got to do with East Africa?!

RD: When you're in this space, or this web, how do you stop to then make the work?

EM: You never stop, you never stop.

RD: This is the thing.

EM: That's the whole point.

RD: I describe it as a pause. I think about it through grammar: I'm never desiring a 'full stop'. So to push against that, I want commas; I want pauses. It's still a point of reflection – that's a good word for it...

EM: Yes, I think sometimes you know for yourself that it's just not right for the piece that you're trying to make. It's not that you slam it into a wall and that's it or you tear up your manuscripts... I've got notepads filled with ideas from years back and I think 'well I never did anything with that idea', but you look back and see that you can do something with it now, or you have new ideas so actually it never stopped. It's a pause, and I really liked what you said: it's a comma, where it slightly shifts or you move in a different direction because what you started with doesn't quite fit where you are now. And that's fine because you're parking it for a moment. In the old fashioned way of saying it: it's on the back burner, the heat is not off but it's on low. You'll know when to take it off or turn up the heat. Some things have to stay on low for a while because they spark other things.

RD: I agree. Even with working sculpturally there are so many works where people ask "when did you get this?" – whether the 'this' is the found objects in an assemblage or the idea itself – and it could be around two years prior. It's been in my studio and I've had to stare it out and it's had to stare me out. I've needed to just be amongst it and move around it by having it on this low heat. I really love a phrasing that Fred Moten had whilst in conversation with Simone (White) where he was talking about having his mother's tongue in his mouth. Most are gagged by the physical idea of that, yet once it settles as a poethic they can come to where I immediately felt which was: this is it! I'm thinking about how best to describe this title I'd been given of being a 'research based artist' and realising this is actually just a natural confluence to have someone's tongue in your mouth: I have my mothers, all my friends, plus the guy from the corner shop's tongue in my mouth. His mannerism comes into my writing – how do I cite that! Perhaps there's a point where citing fails experience. Why does he not get cited when Saidiya (Hartman), for example, gets to be? There are all these different angles that point to the same point.

EM: Are you talking about the hierarchy of importance?

RD: I think it goes into a hierarchy as you're announcing an importance but also you're not denouncing an importance.

EM: Yeah.

RD: My mum would be cited in everything I do and would need to be, as formation stands, as well as my grandma. It's in terms of using this visualisation of the tongue that allows me to think about thick language. How thick language is, is the definition of poethics: the thickened 'h' in poetics. Something has to be done to synthesise from that space. Something has to drain the tongues from my mouth so I can speak! Having this pause provides a point of communication to digest all of these things we acquire by living. I have to eat the tongues sometimes.

EM: You have to eat the tongues but also that frees you up to do other things. It helps you speak more clearly as well. Also, depending on the tongue or who that tongue belongs to; you draw the best of the tongue from that person. That person is helping you. That's a really interesting idea in terms of the guy in the cornershop and how they affect you, or not. Some things are publicly cited and some things are not. That doesn't mean you haven't cited them.

RD: Right. Or shown respect to them.

EM: Exactly. There are people in my life that do come up in my work, not because I've intentionally done that; they've just emerged. I know a lot of things I've done as a vocal improviser stems from communicating with a family member who has problems verbalising things. I've grown up with that person all my life: what I've heard, what they've told me and how we communicate is very special. I'm not always enacting it but I know that it has helped shape and form how I work with text, how I communicate using language or not using language, or how I deconstruct language. That's why often I don't use text in my work but people understand what I'm trying to convey. We've all found ourselves in that situation, particularly in a country where you don't speak the language. You're always reading body language to figure out who looks friendly enough to go up to to ask the way. But you don't just go up to anyone: you really look! I had a friend who was like "Why do people always come up to me for directions?" Are you that person as well?

RD: I feel like people always come up to me for a chat. (laughter)

EM: That's nice, because you have a friendly face and you don't look like someone who's going to cuss them out. You look interesting, that's why!

RD: I'll take that, I look interesting.

EM: When you can pause but keep the energy – that's what I really wanted to work more on. So that, if you're not speaking, you're not not in the piece. There's a difference because the audience can tell as your body language suggests it. You don't have to be directly engaged but you can still be switched on, and that's what I'm talking about; the energy in your own silence or your own pause. Because it's a three way conversation that's going on or it's a three way engagement and sharing of ideas. That's what we do. Look, we're talking and you're not speaking but you're engaged and just being polite. (laughter) Also, there's that moment where everybody is talking together trying to get their point across and that's also exciting. We've all been in a situation, and it doesn't even have to be an argument, but it's all a bit 'ahhh, everybody's got something to say, ahhh!' and you're all spoken out. Then someone just says something and it's done in a very calm way which creates this 'oh yeah, yeah!' energy. It can also be grandparents, an elder.

RD: Which, again goes back to points of hierarchy and points of respect. I think that really makes me think about a question I have for you, which is, when does performance end, and begin when it comes to your day-to-day life? What you're talking about, with these fissures of communication and conversation, are in the day-to-day as we naturally talk over each other, right? It's really interesting when you're in a space and that is performed – I don't think that's really done in opera. Instead it's very rigid, like 'this is your line, this is this person's line' unless there is a song where harmonising comes in which is still a prescribed point of playing. How do you feel performance begins and ends for yourself? There's probably a prescription of 'performance artists are more dramatic than other people', but I've found they're not always. (laughter)

EM: That is something because from a very practical point of view I think the performance starts for me on my journey to wherever I'm going. Or it can start when I'm preparing myself in a warm up where I get myself in a headspace. When I eat is also part of that, because I need to know that I've eaten and had something to drink then I've got the energy I will need. Also, applying make-up… It starts then, but really you would have started it before you've left your house. You're in that mode, even if you do look at your phone or answer a question you're not really there because you've got something to do.

You're presenting a work and so you just have to get yourself into that mindset. And you will know how much time you need.

RD: But you know the more you do it as well.

EM: Absolutely.

RD: Because at the beginning you could feel you need a certain amount of time, but then there's frustration and confusion where you fall out of yourself because you think 'well wait, I should know myself, the time that I have and the time that I own'.

EM: Well we're always learning about ourselves. I'm learning new skills about how to work with my time everyday. I just need a space where I can be quiet. I'll need a warm up so I'll find a space – I don't care if it's a broom cupboard. With my last show there wasn't a set space; there was a dressing room shared with four singers and a piano. Two toilets in this room, both had showers and we all took it in turns to warm up in there. But it was funny because we didn't have a schedule. It was whenever someone needed to just check something they went in there. You'd be in the dressing room and you'd hear two people singing two different things as they were warming up. When you're doing it you're really in your own headspace.

RD: You've got to channel that space. I feel like that brings us back to sound through sound making and sound balancing. We were talking about how, in this world we're getting accosted by sound and sonic interruption all the time. Somehow it just brings me to the 'nothingness' and this 'No Thing' that was repeated in the libretto. I have been thinking about 'nothingness' (in relation to blackness and nothingness), which Moten brings forward. Thinking about non-space and also being prescribed a non-space within inhabiting a black body. How to carve out space and how to carve out space amongst the noise of a point of non-respect: so, how do you frame for self through that. Do you think about that in relation to blackness in terms of carving out sound?

EM: This is really interesting because I understand that notion, but I've not intentionally gone out to carve that space because I always knew that it was there. I think that's because of the way I've been brought up. I know it's been attacked and there have been attempts to rob me of it but I've never allowed it. And I realise I haven't. Even now I know that if someone were to take that from me they would try but they can't because I've just built this protective space around me. It's my armour. I'm not saying I go out and I'm fierce all the time, it's not all blazing up! I feel very safe in there and know they can't touch me, they can't touch me. This is why I'm really interested in the work and research you're doing because writers like Moten are very specific to the American experience but it's really not the same as what we've experienced. It's a very different history, a very different approach... We know more about what's going on there, than they know about what's going on here. We are coming from an Afro-Caribbean heritage. There's more mix, interracial mixing from what's gone on, also because of what's happened in the Caribbean. I think that we, as Black British people, have to embrace, understand, acknowledge and celebrate our own heritage and find the answers to the questions and spaces. Because we know that it is under threat.

RD: Absolutely.

EM: It's being done in a very British way. We've talked about these things and we're very aware of it, therefore it has to be handled differently in order to dismantle that.

RD: Agreed. What is one way of handling this hyper-space of nuance? For example, to give context to my American friends on the contrast of British racism I'll say: "Someone will slam the door in your face in the US, whereas here the door will just continuously not be left open for you; so instead it becomes a psychological tuning into disdain." This no thing, this nothing. I think that that's a question that I desire to answer more: as well as saying that we have this different experience, how can we speak to that for both the Black British and those who are trying to understand that, because it can be very psychologically frustrating.

EM: I think what's happened in the past with the first generation of black Britons – as in modern black Britons particularly coming out of the Roots and Dub culture, or people like Olive Morris – where the door was not quite left open, they took the door and then they opened it. In my mind that's how I've carved out my space. I knew that for the kind of music I wanted to make and the kind of singing I wanted to do that that would be very hard for me. People want to pigeonhole you so I've made my own scene. I knew that firstly I needed to express what I needed to express and secondly if I tried to go down one root they weren't going to get what I'm doing, so okay... I'll just do it! Because I need to do it!

You do come across people who will support you and they're coming from these institutions, but it's seeking out those like-minded folks who are daring, brave enough and conscious enough to do that. I think it's really important that we don't pull the ladder up behind us because we've been given an opportunity. If the door looks like it's being closed and we choose to open that door, we must wedge it and keep it open.

RD: Yes, but we're still building that wedge, I think that's really interesting. This comes back to the trickster. In the zine I made for the Serpentine hand out, I talked about the natural abstract means of existence that's due to the linearity of 'doors being open' for whiteness, for example, and the carriages of life for them being entered very easily. A blackness, or extending that – a non-whiteness – has this point of abstraction. I talk about having to find something else that could be the key for that door, like an available doorstop or another kind of wedge that you'll have to make. It could be a tongue, like for the poets.

I'm reading (Kamau) Braithwaite's *Roots* right now as a point of engaging with Caribbean literature and how to continue this point of poethics by bringing language to the concept of how it is innate in us. It was really interesting reading what he's saying, just like you're saying, about the first generation. To me they're speaking so much about the diaspora but they're giving the first language to the diaspora as we/it stands now. This brings it back to the way that both (Stuart) Hall and Braithwaite put it, in that they state that just being Caribbean is naturally being this fluctuated, abstracted, multi-layered society and group of people. Framing how it starts there and leads to where we are now; that's been most interesting to see through these two eloquent voices.

EM: Absolutely! What fascinates me is what they're saying has been embraced much more over the last maybe 10 years, and it's part of this new canon of poethics, ideas and philosophy. Before they kind of got sidelined. It's not that it's fashionable, it's just so relevant and what we need: these voices! They have made the path but before we just haven't seen it as it had been obscured or hidden. That's what I would say is the positive that has come out of the Black Lives Matter movement; this energy, this strength and decision to not be quiet. I don't care if this is going to piss you off! You're going to hear it anyway and you're not going to stop. They can't stop it now.

RD: No one told me about Braithwaite. I found him through reading someone else! There are so many of these things and people that I've picked up myself, just as a kid who was a reader as well as this only child who had to have a book, you know what I mean? I feel like there's also another side of it with the Black Lives Matter movement resurgence and uprising, where actually maybe there are members of us who have already been saying this. Let me go find these people – I don't want to listen to whiteness anymore. There has to be others. And when you do find one (e.g. I'm reading June Jordan and Derek Walcott right now in a joint Caribbean analysis) then you find another. That is being picked up from Black Lives Matter in a sense that there are literary canons being revealed. I found a Caribbean poetry group and I'm still finding out who they all are. It has been written about! The Francophone countries have had a stronghold on theory and philosophy. I'm finding out that some of them wrote poetry also and am trying to source their chapbooks. Then it just goes back to the archive and ephemera, and how frustrating it can be to find these tangible histories to (re)build that knowledge.

EM: Absolutely. I think about some of these modern writers like Bernadine Everisto who I've known about for years but who's work

I've never actually read, not because I didn't think she was any good – I just hadn't read her. She's used winning the (2019 Booker) prize to force a change. What happened to George Floyd has forced an acceleration of change. Even if people didn't want it, they had to. Because anyone who put a black square on social media in solidarity is now being held accountable. It terrifies a lot of people, it has brought joy to many, and it has opened up the canon to so many different people, especially to younger generations. Also the question of 'why was this obscured? Why didn't I know about this? I've studied literature, how did I not know…?'

RD: That's me in every book, I'm like, 'what? How dare I not know!'

(laughter)

EM: This is it. When I was researching *sweet tooth* I thought I needed to have a historical consultant and that was really helpful for me. I was watching some programme on iPlayer about (Horatio) Nelson in the Caribbean – it was really a terrible BBC program, but it was interesting. There was a hurricane that revealed all these bones of the English naval officers on a beach in Antigua, who'd died because of the tropical heat. They shouldn't have been there in the first place. There were all of these talking heads in this doc and there was a guy who was the president of the Caribbean historical site, he was a white guy yet what he said was quite interesting. I took his name down, Christo, and googled him and it revealed he was at Southampton University. He became the historical consultant for *sweet tooth* because his PhD was on a slaveholder in Jamaica. He'd never been to the Caribbean in his life but just went on a 6 month research trip to Jamaica! He was able to do that and he was very aware of his ability. I started talking to him about his experiences there and how he felt being a minority. He said he didn't want to write his PhD on this person because he'd owned enslaved Africans on three plantations. Instead it was a very factual and helpful piece of writing that I was able to use to expose the inhumanities Christo had revealed from this slave owner's diary! It talks about the slave owner's paranoia of things falling apart and losing his wealth. The reason why I mention Christo is because he said, "do you know the work of Kamau Braithwaite?" He'd met him before and then bought me a book of poetry by him. I could not believe I didn't know anything about Braithwaite. In the same way I didn't know anything about Una Marson, the first black producer at the BBC in the 40's. These people are iconoclasts. They've paved the way for what you're doing and for what I'm doing now. They weren't on the fringe, they were very much involved in changing things.

RD: There's so much that comes from what you've just said. Firstly, that idea of fringe is what irks me, as a person can be deemed as 'fringe' because of how society has chosen to remember them. That is so frustrating. That's where I form such a focus when I'm teaching students. I tell them, "have a friend come and photograph you – as doing this creates respect for your archive now, not later." Society might not respect it now or later. So how do you build an archive as a living artist?

I want to come back to Christo – you stating he's a conscious person and how he was looking at a slave owner. I was in this poetry group and there were so many people who were studying colonialism, so many white people, where they also had someone like Kobena Mercer as their advisor and I thought that was amazing, what an opportunity! The point I'm trying to make, and also question is that sitting in this group, hearing these people have all these discussions of colonialism, I felt that many were not actually coming from a point of view of how whiteness stands within colonialism: how that plays out, what is it to be a 'conscious person' but to instantly imbed yourself for 6 months in a Black place, how does that come to a full version of conscious? Sure there is a version of consciousness in talking about this slavemaster 'owner' but then perhaps there isn't, because you're focusing on this person. What about focusing on the people who've come from that? And the people who were greatly affected by that? What is conscious, is it also funding a black person to go back and do that root work alongside you, is that true conscious? Where and how in the ontic of your reality, does that play into a conscious? Because you're doing an ontology of blackness research no matter what.

EM: That is not a question for me, that's a question for Christo.

RD: I think it's a part of the same discussion.

EM: Absolutely and it's a question that I did kind of pose to him, which is why I took the material. We had very interesting conversations about this. It was a frustration because historically, when you look at what's available, there are things that have survived in the archive that give us these traces of our forebearers that they weren't allowed to express themselves artistically.
You won't see carvings, paintings, or things that show an artistic expression. But what has survived is the big drum tradition. What has survived is the nation language that has been born out of this. What has survived are the songs. What has survived is the movement; the dance. These things which still influence. As Black British people we can't hear pop music without knowing where that inspiration's coming from. You can't listen to either grime or anything that has a reference to drum and bass. I hate Ed Sheeran but you cannot listen to him and forget he's pulling from that.

RD: Oh yeah, I hear jungle aspects in Ed Sheeran!

EM: You hear the jungle but where is that coming from? We can hear that and there are people who are not black who acknowledge it and say that being white allows them a privilege and a kind of access to these kinds of music.

RD: Let's actually bring that into blackness and within a colourism spectrum too, which is something both of us can speak to from different vantage points.

EM: Yes.

RD: What do you feel is something that maybe you are in engagement with, in terms of your placeholder in a colourism conversation? Whether in its broadest sense, through a subject matter or your whole life as a practice, etc.

EM: I feel there is a real responsibility. The work I do is the work I do and I think it's always going to critique this systemic racism and injustice. I also have to bring class into it and how you mentioned earlier that class is discussed more than race. I mean, we're looking at this Tory leadership race now and there's this whole big thing about 'there's so many ethnic minorities who want to be Prime Minister, how could that be?' And it's like they're Asian and they're Black, but we're not alike. Politically we're not alike: they are not going to represent me. They want power. They're not fit to have power because they desire it – so that puts me off straight away. They're not activists, they're not changing anything, instead, they're here to maintain the status quo. We don't have the same values so I feel that, for me, I need to create work and keep pushing, questioning and calling these things out. I'm not a politician, I'm not a public speaker. I'm very interested in history and how that's affecting what we're doing now, as well as how it will affect our futures, and how to readdress that. That's why I took the information for *sweet tooth*; the very cold dry facts and said that's about this person. I'm interested in the people that were exploited. Let's honour them; their strength and the fact that they're survivors because if they hadn't, I wouldn't be here. You wouldn't be here. We'd exist in a different way if it hadn't happened at all. I try to remind myself of these things. I feel that there is a responsibility to support, and to be a part of this collective. We support each other.

RD: Do you think about it in terms of a quota?

EM: Not really. Despite everything, people kind of know who I am and what I'm doing. I think when you're presenting and you get this profile, there's a level of responsibility in how you handle that and how you help others gain access. So I don't have a quota as you just don't know. Because your influence is also not just to the black community, other people will also be inspired by what you do. It is important to remember that.

Do you feel that you've not reached your audience if you do a piece and the viewers are predominantly white? Do you think you have failed?

RD: No, I don't think I have failed but I think it should ignite a concentration and conversation of how that audience is brought to a space. In terms of both PR/ communication output and then also positions of access. I'm not necessarily Jeremy O'Harris' audience but I was really intrigued by his idea for a 'Black Out' audience, which I'm sure isn't a new concept but he has now given a term to it. There's this position for one night to be a completely black audience. However, that still didn't happen as I went to a performance where some people had their white partners, which is their prerogative. Yet, the seeking out and the stating is really important as then you're really holding the door and also shouting out from it: come in!

EM: Yeah, but people may not want to hear it.

RD: They may not want to hear it, but I think there are definitely avenues of how you can angle and direct that voice. You can know that you have attempted that. There are spaces that offer discounted tickets for minority ethnicities. That's a point of access that feels amazing because what we're talking about is knowing how to cross the threshold.

EM: I think that this is a completely different thing. I don't think money has anything to do with it.

RD: You think?

EM: Not at all. I know why I'm saying this because I know how much we can spend on ourselves. Whether it's on our hair and clothes or tickets to go and see your favourite artist – which is much more expensive than anything you and I will do. That audience will spend because people go to watch what they think they'll enjoy, and I respect that choice. Last weekend there were young people at the Wireless festival carnage. It was like the United Colours of Benetton, but predominantly black. Everybody was showing out and good for them because it was Cardi B, SZA, Megan the Stallion, someone else…

RD: Summer Walker.

EM: Right: that crowd. Now, some of them played at Glastonbury. That audience was all white because black folk don't do mystic festivals out in the field somewhere where you have to be in a tent and share a toilet with thousands of people.

RD: Even watching those audiences from Wireless I was still surprised that there was a big sea of white people.

EM: And they know the songs more than I do!

RD: They know the songs and they sing along to the expletives! I'm like 'okay you can say that with your full chest – very interesting, very scary, very interesting!' But what you're saying in terms of not paying for it is from a point of position and value. 'Are you valuing this thing as a nourishment of the arts for you this week?'

EM: It's also about education. Earlier we were both lamenting about not knowing about these great writers. Now if you add the great artists, performance artists and musicians... if as a child you are exposed to that, you grow with the thinking 'so that's what happens in this place, or that music happens, or that person does *this* despite it being a little strange'. When you're young you're not critiquing things in the same way. As a child you can absorb football, athletics, pop music and rap music. Even those things weren't accessible when I was younger, like hip hop and rap; when you're much older you can get to that. I'm an old woman so I'm talking about a few years back now!

I've done my improv in a black club in Brixton, right? They loved it when I was doing something a bit more like rhythm and beats, but as soon as I started to veer out I could see their faces go. I wanted to laugh! I was cracking up because I felt like 'well this is alright, they don't do the avant garde'. That's fine. Yet, if they go to a Pentecostal church they're gonna see more of the avant garde there compared to what I do on stage!

RD: That's interesting thinking about the location of the live recording of *sweet tooth*, and how it was playing to the chapel space. Plus the acoustics of that reverberation of self and sonics right?

EM: Yeah, and that night I would say was the first and only time I've played *sweet tooth* where it had more black people there. I think that it's because we were in London. It premiered in Liverpool which had quite a mixed crowd. In London there were many more: people like Ain Bailey came so it was a really good crowd.

RD: People we know.

EM: The energy was different and I'm not gonna lie it felt different. We all could feel it, we didn't have to say it.

RD: Did you feel like you were held by the energy of the understood? The energy of 'I relate'?

EM: It felt that it gave the piece a different kind of energy that was good for it. I did it in Bergen in Norway where there was a group of young people who are not Norwegian born but they're from different parts of the African continent, mainly East Africa but living in Bergen. They were invited into lots of different types of concerts at this particular festival I was performing at and came to *sweet tooth* where they sat front row.

Again, here I could feel from our brothers and sisters that they felt 'someone is talking about the experience, someone is talking about the experience'! We had a chat for about half an hour afterwards and they started to really express how they felt about being in Norway. You talk about tongues: in that moment it felt like this tongue of freedom where we could speak in a very safe space.

RD: I was going to ask about that space being carved out. Had you asked for the space or had the festival said, "we also want you to be in conversation with these young people"?

EM: The festival was really keen on that happening. I didn't know they were going to be there until maybe the day before when I was asked and I said absolutely! I was really touched by it, so I actually felt like 'this piece is not good because I made it; it's good because of what people talk about and how they feel through experiencing it'. To do it in Norway (because Norway has its own colonial history that they're only now acknowledging) was this weird thing because at the end of *sweet tooth* you don't know what to do; do you clap? You can't really woop – it's not that kind of piece! Often people are looking really shaken and tearful so they just have to leave. Yet, in Norway it was almost as though the only thing that they could do was just stand up! Everyone stood up, and then started applauding. It was so moving! I think they just had to release, and from a performer's perspective seeing people just have to release is really powerful because it's clear 'you were in this journey with us'! Because that's the way I work. I kind of grab people on a journey; whether they want it or not, they're coming anyway. It's interesting about the whole 'playing to a particular audience' as of course I want to perform... I would love to bring *sweet tooth* to schools. I suspect that if this was 10-20 years ago you probably could have done it without much fuss and bother. But now because of the way the government has been where they curtail everything it has made it really hard.

RD: You tried and it was really hard?

EM: I had made inquiries. There are a lot of obstacles to it being brought there, but I've felt that actually it's the kind of piece I would take into secondary schools. But I'm not sure if that could happen now...

RD: What about the secondary school that you went to?

EM: The secondary school that I went to has now been closed.

RD: Oh.

EM: It doesn't matter, it was only three bloody hundred years old!

(both laughing)

EM: I was really shocked when I saw! I was like '300 years in 2020 and now it's closing'! It was a C of E [Church of England] school in Tower Hamlets, which is now predominantly Bangladeshi, so parents are not sending their kids to a C of E school. It was dwindling. It wasn't very strict in terms of religion to be honest: my school friends were Hindu, Jewish, Muslim, non-believing and everything else in between.

RD: Tower Hamlets has always been pretty diverse.

EM: Yeah. I think maybe in your generation, and those to come, they will want to embrace things that are more avant garde or a bit more experimental as part of their culture. But also I respect that each community knows what they want to hear!

RD: It's like where culture gets born and framed. Even within my family there is this group of people that are connected by blood, yet my house that I was raised in was an R&B and soul house, whereas most of my cousins had a reggae household. I'd come to a family party and be lost. I'd complain to my mum that 'I don't know this one?' I didn't know it because I had Maxwell, Jill Scott and Tina Marie, you know! I know the top drawer of reggae but I don't know the deep cuts per se!

EM: (laughter) I'm laughing because YES to the references!

RD: It is hilarious: cleaning the house was Luther Vandross and Barry White! That's also something that I bode to a Black culture, meaning some of my American friends had a jazz and soul upbringing as opposed to how the Black British, who are so much more connected to the Caribbean, have reggae and ska. My ex-partner had reggae and I met them with soul and we became the full 'Black' compass together.

(both laughing)

EM: It's so funny!

RD: It's interesting how these points of culture build. Also, the desire to culture reference that comes through my sculpture and painting artworks. Much like the cabinet, 'A Caribbean Ossuary' in my last solo exhibition: so many Caribbean households have one, yet there will be points in an exhibition where I'm speaking solely to my grandma and I's conversations, like the spade works. Some other people can be in the metaphorical room with that conversation, and some other people are really at the window. There's these different leverages of, again, these ontologies of Blackness, that are able to denote different regions of the world. Whether that's lowercase (black) or uppercase (Black), you know?

What is interesting in these points of collaboration, or maybe even breaches in them, is seen through this really great, really old video on YouTube of Tinie Tempah – do you remember him?

EM: Yes, he's still going?

RD: Now he's in real estate. He's a presenter on this TV show called *Extraordinary Extensions* on Channel 4 that came out last year where he reports on people's house extensions. You know what, take your money and be smart with it!

But why I brought him up is that when he was Tinie Tempah, the rapper, the Tate invited him to come visit the Chris Ofili show, and they recorded it. I love this video because I think it's a really important discourse within black class structure, especially how that was being built in the UK at that time. I think that was Chris Ofili's first show there or something. It had the blue series and 'No Woman No Cry', Ofili's infamous painting. Tinie Tempah isn't building around any theory or 'art history' linguistic; he's just responding. He's speaking about seeing Stephen Lawrence's face in the tears, what the colours mean to him... I think that video is so great because it's so important to not prescribe to this idea of a singular reading of an artwork. I see the video as a form of collaboration: Chris Ofili x Tinie Tempah. Two different versions of Black Britishness, let alone two different creative outputs. Both are equally important.

I come from both of those versions. I was in residence in Marseille trying to hold on to my accent yet I was speaking to so many of my American friends so I decided to watch Bridgerton and Top Boy, simultaneously. Bridgerton meets Top Boy is where I exist. I'm from Croydon but I went to school in Surrey. Do you know what I mean?

EM: Yes. (laughter)

RD: It goes back to the idea of an innate Caribbean-ness that we were talking about earlier. These realities of being multifaceted and what can come from these points of collaboration. There's definitely a time and a place for collaboration, and at what point the collaboration comes into a direct interaction, like Chris presumably didn't have Tinie Tempah in the studio but he is in collaboration in a secondary (sense of) space.

EM: There's been a couple of similar programs; mostly with art and then with music. There was one with Goldie on art further back, him talking about Picasso or someone like that, which was quite interesting actually because of the way he was expressing a more personal response to the paintings. Thinking about how you mention collaboration in terms of the *Timeless* album, which people may not like but was a very important moment in drum and bass. The tracks were orchestrated and I was one of the backing singers. I was really sceptical about it, but had the best time because the actual album leant itself very well as an orchestra. He said, "when I created this piece I always had an orchestra in mind, I just didn't have an orchestra at hand." It made sense musically. It was one of the loudest nights I've ever experienced at the Festival Hall and it was sold out. It was a completely diverse audience because that scene was racially mixed. People were smoking joints and everyone was a bit older. They'd left the kids at home and were reliving back in the day. It had a really friendly vibe. As soon as the orchestra walked on, I'll never forget, everyone started screaming and cheering and whooping and we hadn't even played a note yet!

(both laughing)

RD: That sounds magical.

EM: It was magical. If it ever happens again, I'll let you know! It's a gig that, despite being something that is not my world, I actually loved. It was done with a lot of integrity. Goldie's changed his life, he's had a particular background where it may not have ended up this way, had his brushes with the law... so it's an interesting story. That feels very British to me in a positive way.

I'm intrigued about your family and how they respond to your work? Because I don't know if there is another artist in your family, so you stand out anyway!

RD: What I am really fortunate to have is a family who lets me go 'off into the woods' in their terms. That's a huge privilege and so many families do not have that point of freedom and ability to just go off and wonder. But no – my family aren't artists, they also don't have their own companies. They've pretty much always worked from salary jobs, usually in some kind of labour to the government. That makes me think of how writing an invoice was something I had to learn to do myself.

I describe it as 'looking into present histories', in a sense that my grandma and grandad are both living, and I'm thinking about their generation and that movement. I always read 'movement' as both a dance/gesture but also as the possession of black movement politically.

EM: Of course.

RD: Which you definitely did speak to in *sweet tooth*. That movement for me and being able to be in conversation with a present generation is important. Not that they're always forthcoming in their stories – we as a family have literally only been able to have a direct question and answer session with my grandma once – as I think it's quite harrowing in this reality of difference that holds so much, for her especially. It's about finding a space in that place. I'd said to my family, "we need to talk to grandma about this because she is grand-ma."

EM: How old is she?

RD: She is 78. I've lived with my grandma on and off throughout my life so I'm super close with her and she's one of my favourite family members. She's a Virgo which is also fab.

I took her on the last day of my exhibition at my gallery, Soft Opening, to walk through the show. There are things that I read from the conversations we've had, or readings from the texts that I work through, for example Sam Selvon's 'The Lonely Londoners'. It's a great narrative on this point of arrival that the generation of my grandparents don't often directly speak about, because it was a very difficult and painful time. The book allowed me to have a point of entry with my grandma as I'd ask "was this really said at this time or did this really happen?" you know, and sometimes it comes to a difficult head. For example, in part of the book one of the characters complains that he got called a 'wog', or something along those lines, and the protagonist starts to list the other 'things' that you're going to get called. In this list it got to 'spade' which struck me. I remember going to my grandma and asking, "did you get called a spade?" and she says, "yeah" and promptly moved on with the conversation, and her day. That is also a point of how in her/their histories you did have to move on with the day, and these are still present histories of being called something or seeing the white guy in a concert next to you sing shouting the word, "nigger!" and being like 'I'm trying to enjoy myself but now I have to address that, or do I have to address you? Will I decide to do that? Will I take myself out of this present fun? Do I have the choice now that moment has happened? What is this?' That point of play and position is changing the detriment it can create, but it's still in that linguistic of absolving a self. I'm really glad that I can speak with her and I really found it important to be able to bring her to the show in London. I know Saturdays are her market days and she always busies herself – she goes to Zumba everyday!

EM: Fantastic.

RD: She's fab. It is still research work. It is engagement with these writers and people who brought language to those time periods and then can support this language. We're going back to language, which I think is also a nice way to end as well. I'm super grateful to the moments my grandma gives and don't expect her to have all the language. She isn't that kind of person and that's also a different reality of being in this society: Windrush versus descendent Black British.

EM: Her being is that language.

RD: Definitely.

EM: Who she is is that language she doesn't even have to do anything; it's how she is. She's sharing it with you, sometimes we just don't see it. Or we do, but we haven't had time to process it. Quite often it's afterwards when they've travelled somewhere and we have to meet them further down the line. That's where we realise 'okay that's what she meant by that...' It's a lifelong search.

RD: It really is. It needs to be said that it's a lifelong research. It has two sides like a boat (that metaphor balances for many reasons of course!): one is to acknowledge that this is lifelong research, but the second is to also acknowledge that it is about your life and so sit with that, allow that to be buoyant in that space and be present in that time.

Was there anything else that you wanted to say to close?

EM: I think the achievements of *Catgut* are really tremendous with the time that you had, what you embraced and what you did. I've said from just looking at it, from a slightly critical eye if I can...

RD: I love critique, this is my favourite. That's why we're now friends. (laughter)

EM: Okay. I think if you'd had a little bit more time there are the things you would have come to.

RD: To refine and embody more right?

EM: Yes! But you should really try to do it again.

RD: You think?

EM: Yeah, definitely.

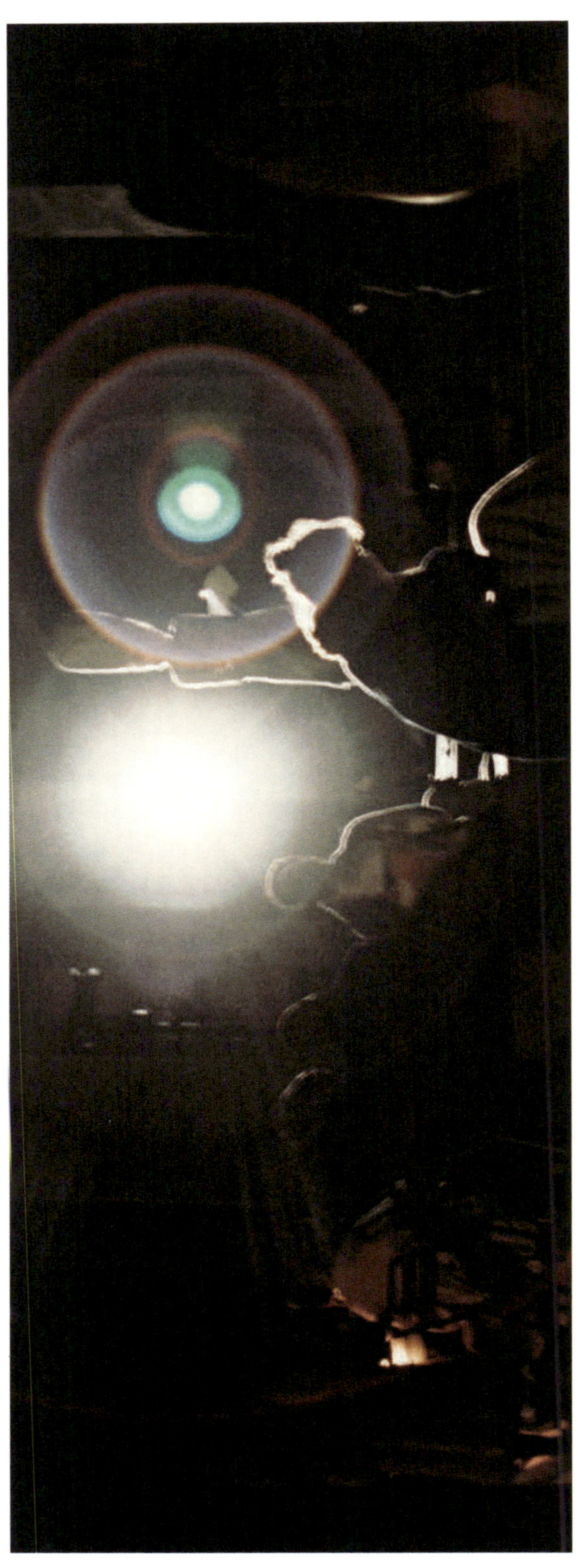

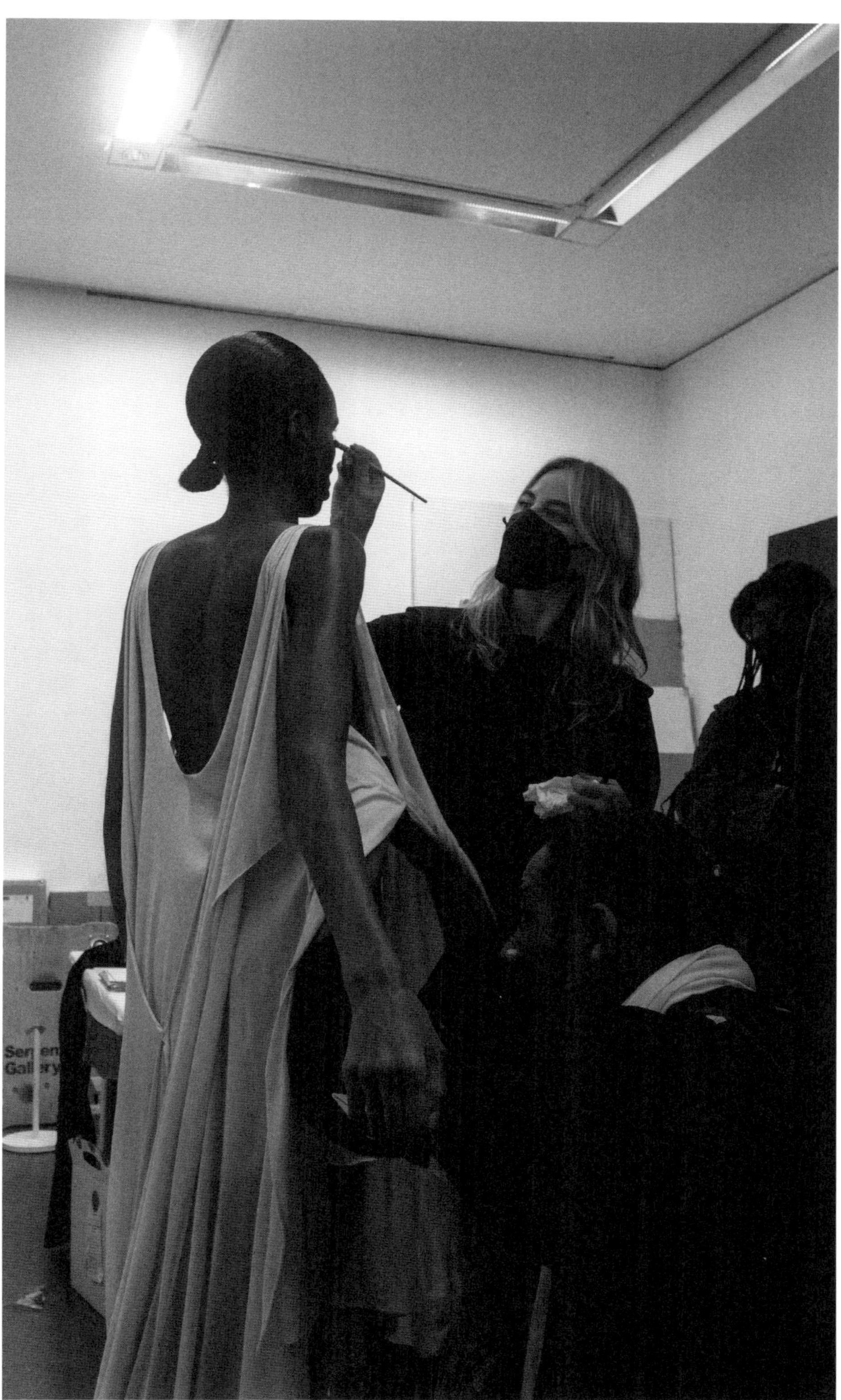

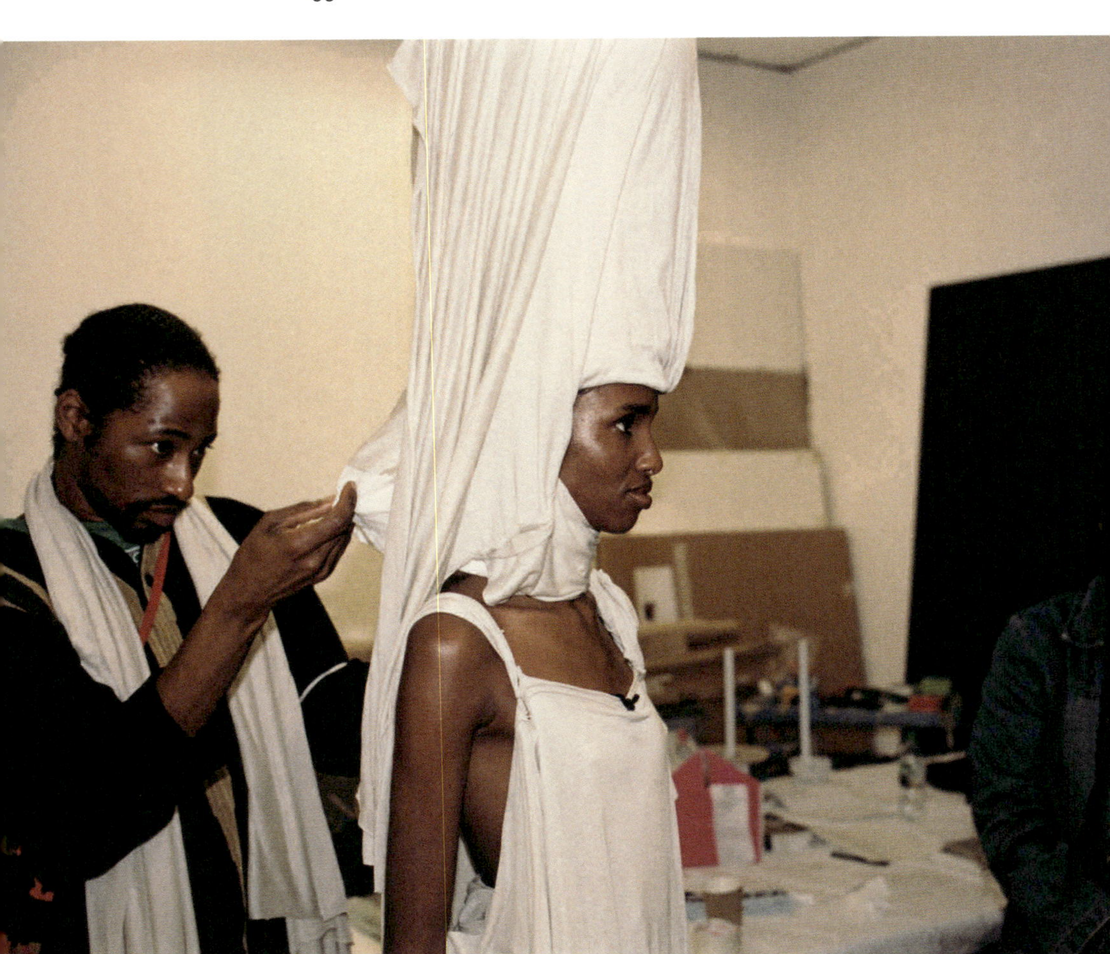

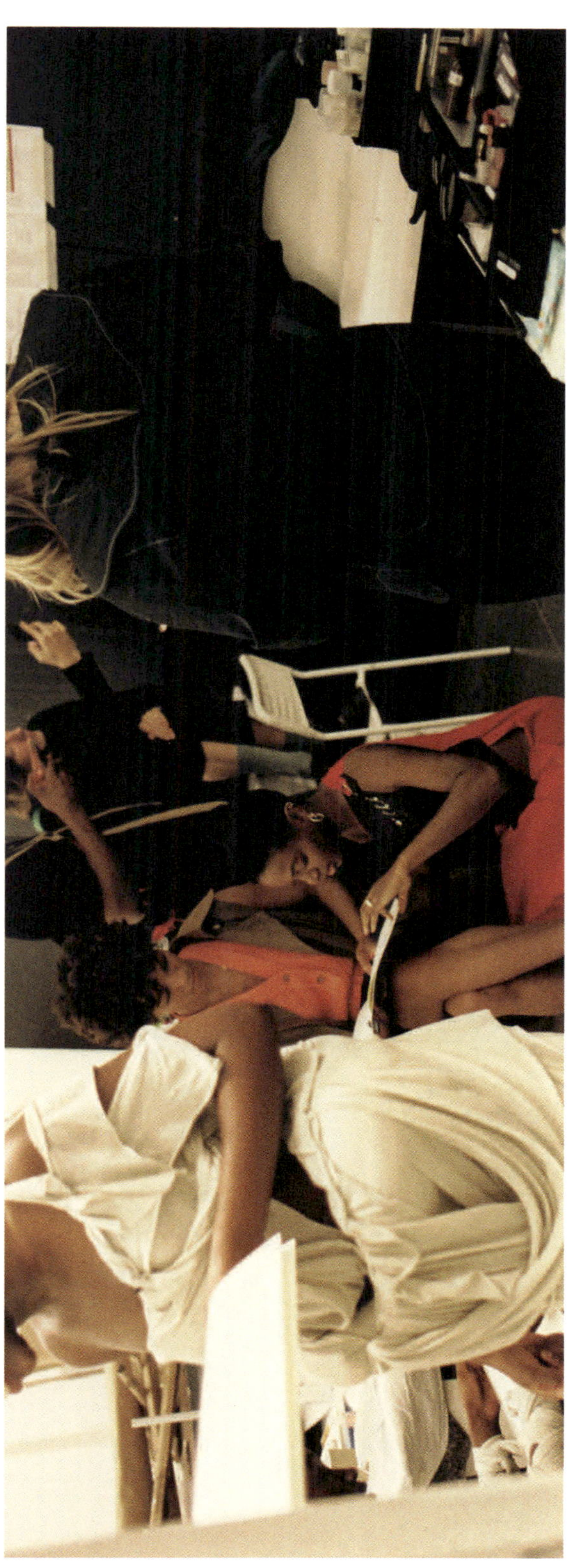

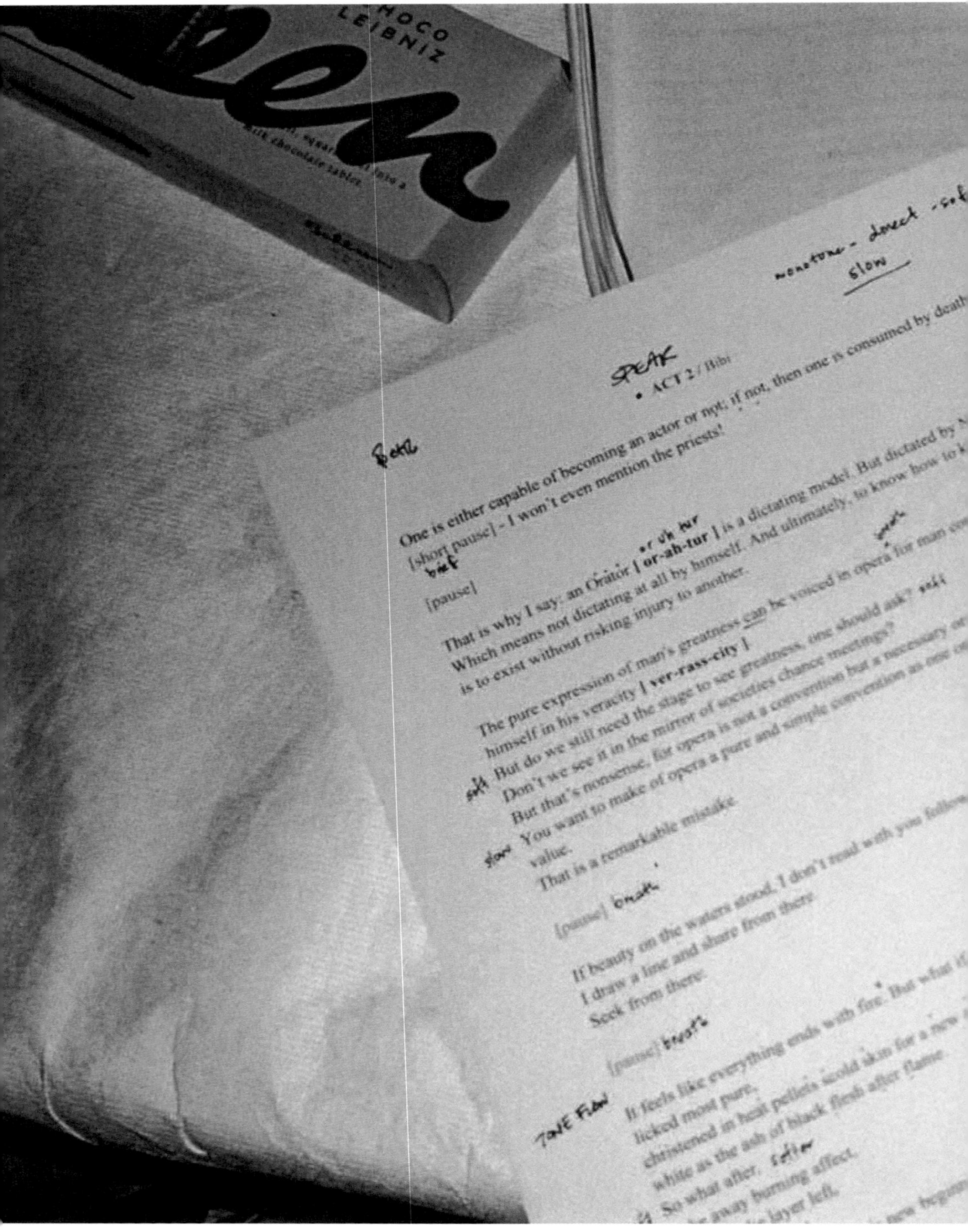
CHOCO
LEIBNIZ
milk chocolate tablet
slow
SPEAK
• ACT 2 / Bibi
One is either capable of becoming an actor or not; if not, then one is consumed by death
[short pause] - I won't even mention the priests!
[pause]
That is why I say: an Orator | or-ah-tur | is a dictating model. But dictated by
Which means not dictating at all by himself. And ultimately, to know how to
is to exist without risking injury to another.
The pure expression of man's greatness can be voiced in opera for man
himself in his veracity | ver-rass-city |
But do we still need the stage to see greatness, one should ask?
Don't we see it in the mirror of societies chance meetings?
But that's nonsense, for opera is not a convention but a necessary
You want to make of opera a pure and simple convention as one
value.
That is a remarkable mistake
[pause]
If beauty on the waters stood, I don't read with you
I draw a line and share from there
Seek from there.
[pause]
TONE FLOW
It feels like everything ends with fire. But what if
licked most pure,
christened in heat pellets scold skin for a new
white as the ash of black flesh after flame.
So what after,
away burning affect.
layer left.

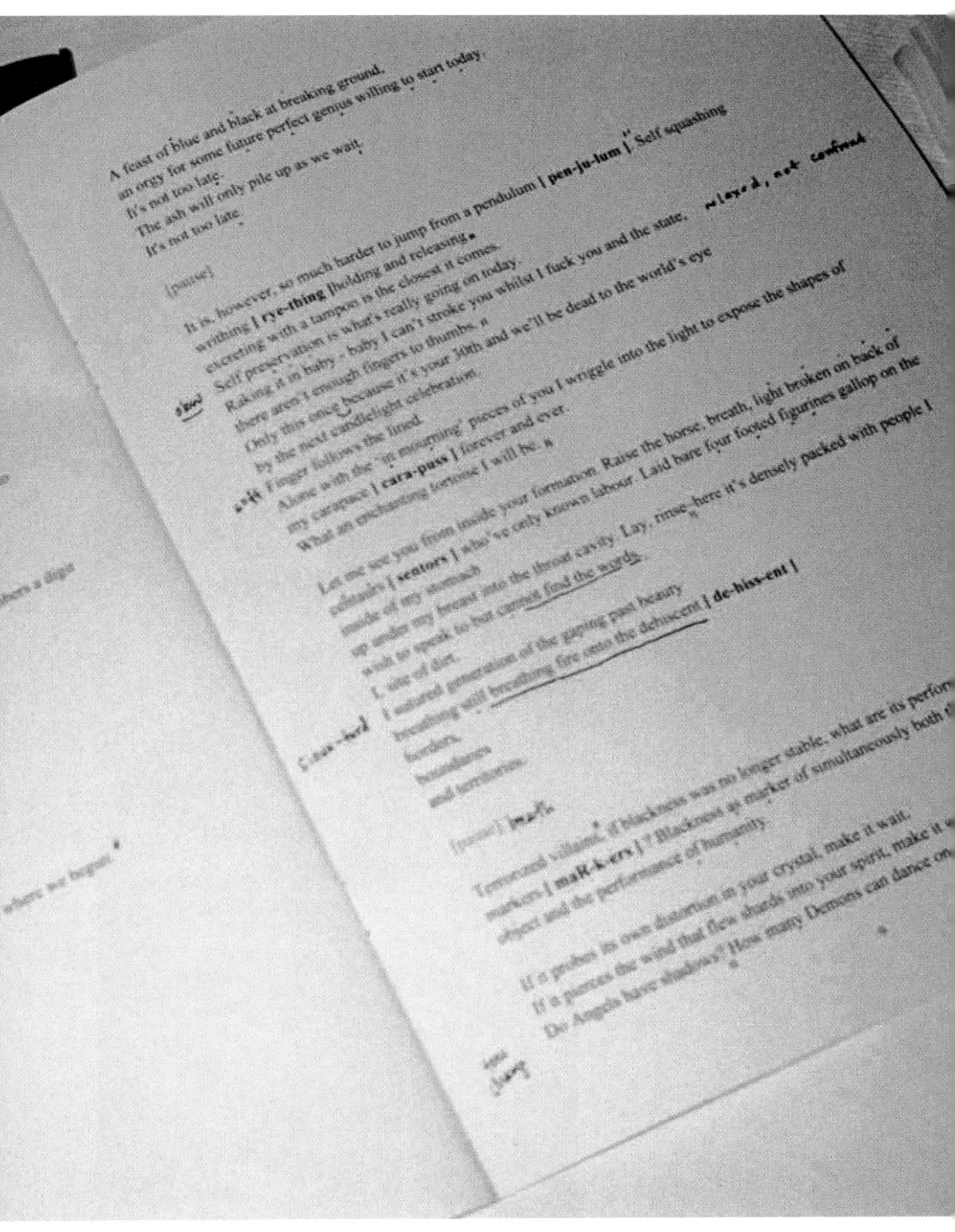

A feast of blue and black at breaking ground,
an orgy for some future perfect genius willing to start today.
It's not too late.
The ash will only pile up as we wait.
It's not too late.

[pause]

It is, however, so much harder to jump from a pendulum | **pen-ju-lum** |. Self squashing
writhing | **rye-thing** | holding and releasing.
excreting with a tampon is the closest it comes.
Self preservation is what's really going on today.
Raking it in baby - baby I can't stroke you whilst I fuck you and the state.
there aren't enough fingers to thumbs.
Only this once because it's your 30th and we'll be dead to the world's eye
by the next candlelight celebration.
Finger follows the lined.
Alone with the 'in mourning' pieces of you I wriggle into the light to expose the shapes of
my carapace | **cara-puss** | forever and ever.
What an enchanting tortoise I will be.

Let me see you from inside your formation. Raise the horse, breath, light broken on back of
celestials | **sentors** | who've only known labour. Laid bare four footed figurines gallop on the
inside of my stomach
up under my breast into the throat cavity. Lay, rinse, here it's densely packed with people I
wish to speak to but cannot find the words.
[site of dirt
[saturated generation of the gaping past beauty
breathing still breathing fire onto the dehiscent | **de-hiss-ent** |
borders,
boundaries
and territories.

[pause]

Terrorized villains, if blackness was no longer stable, what are its perfor
markers | **mar-k-ers** |? Blackness as marker of simultaneously both th
object and the performance of humanity.

If it probes its own distortion in your crystal, make it wait.
If it pierces the wind that flew shards into your spirit, make it w
Do Angels have shadows? How many Demons can dance on

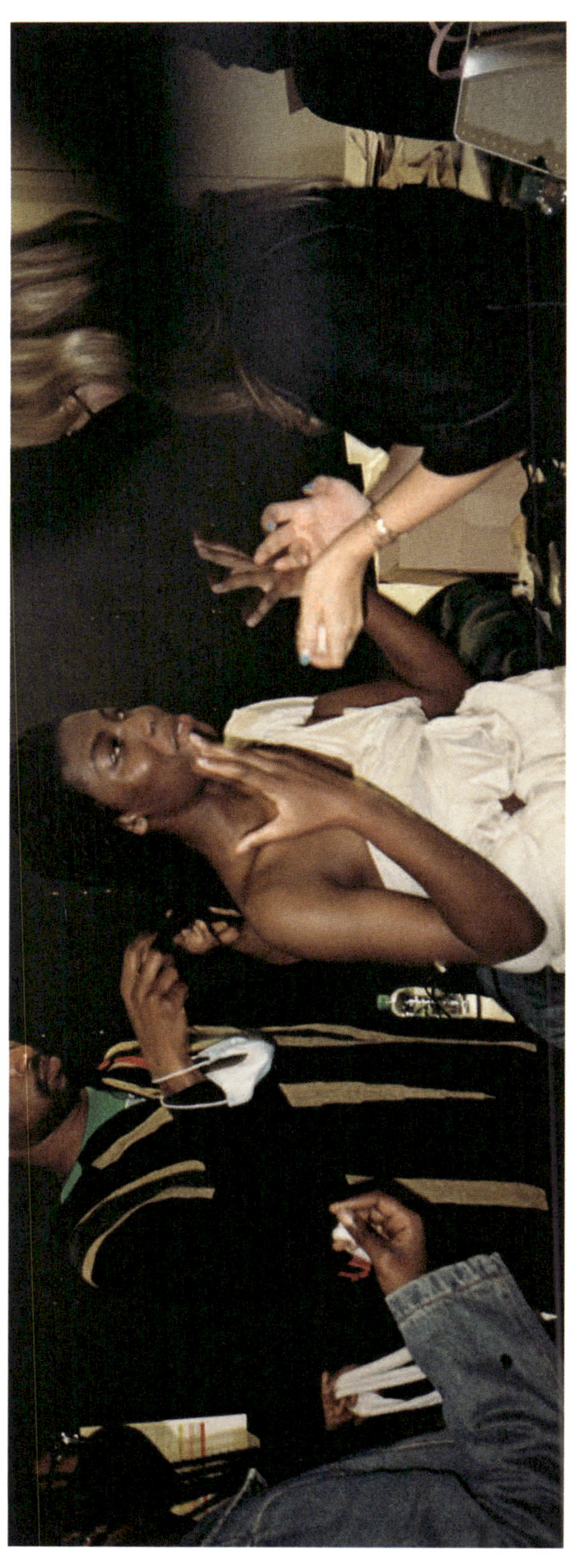

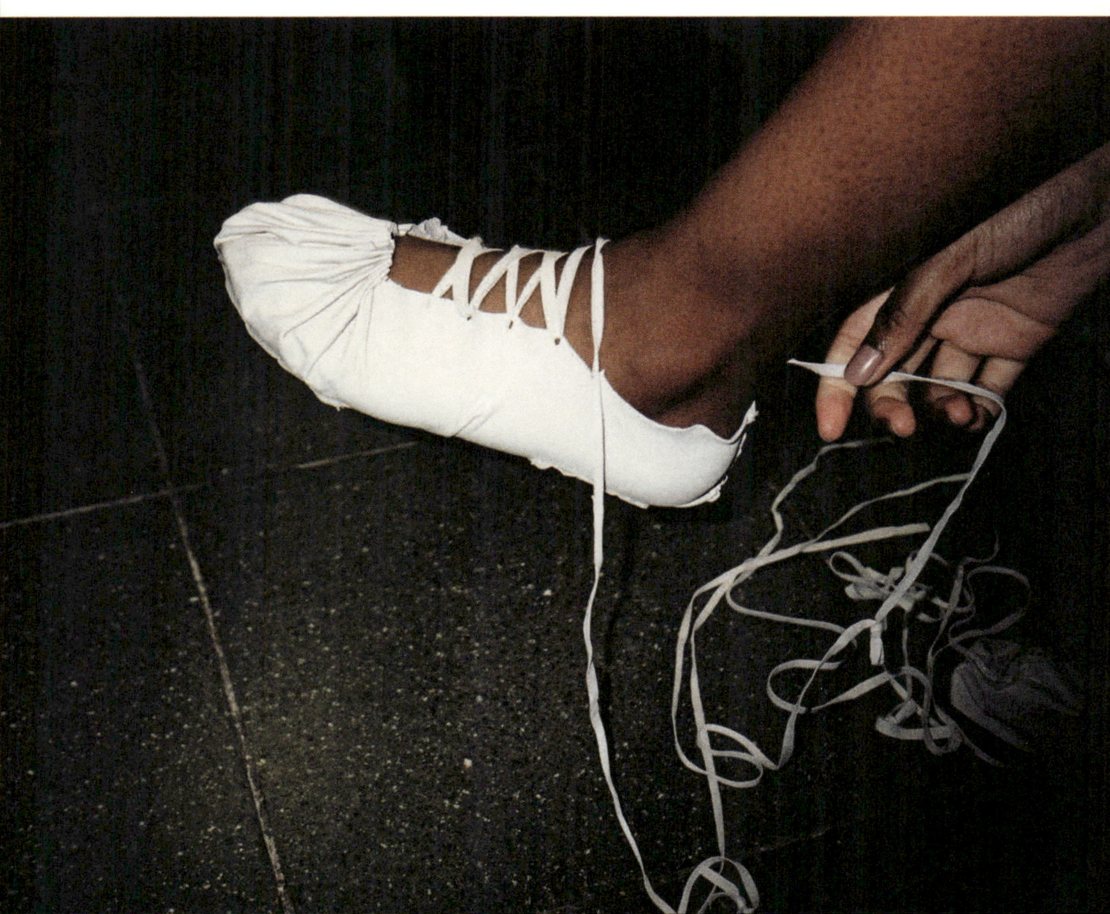

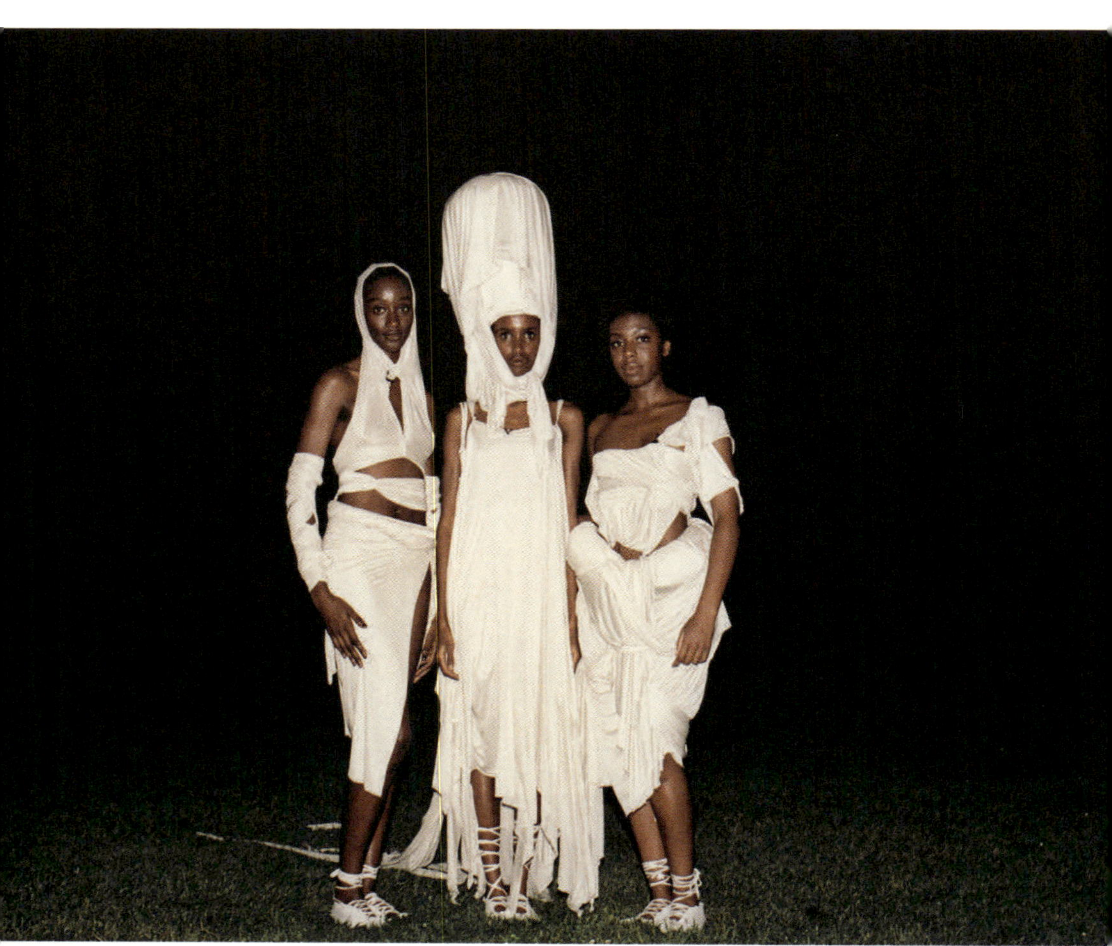

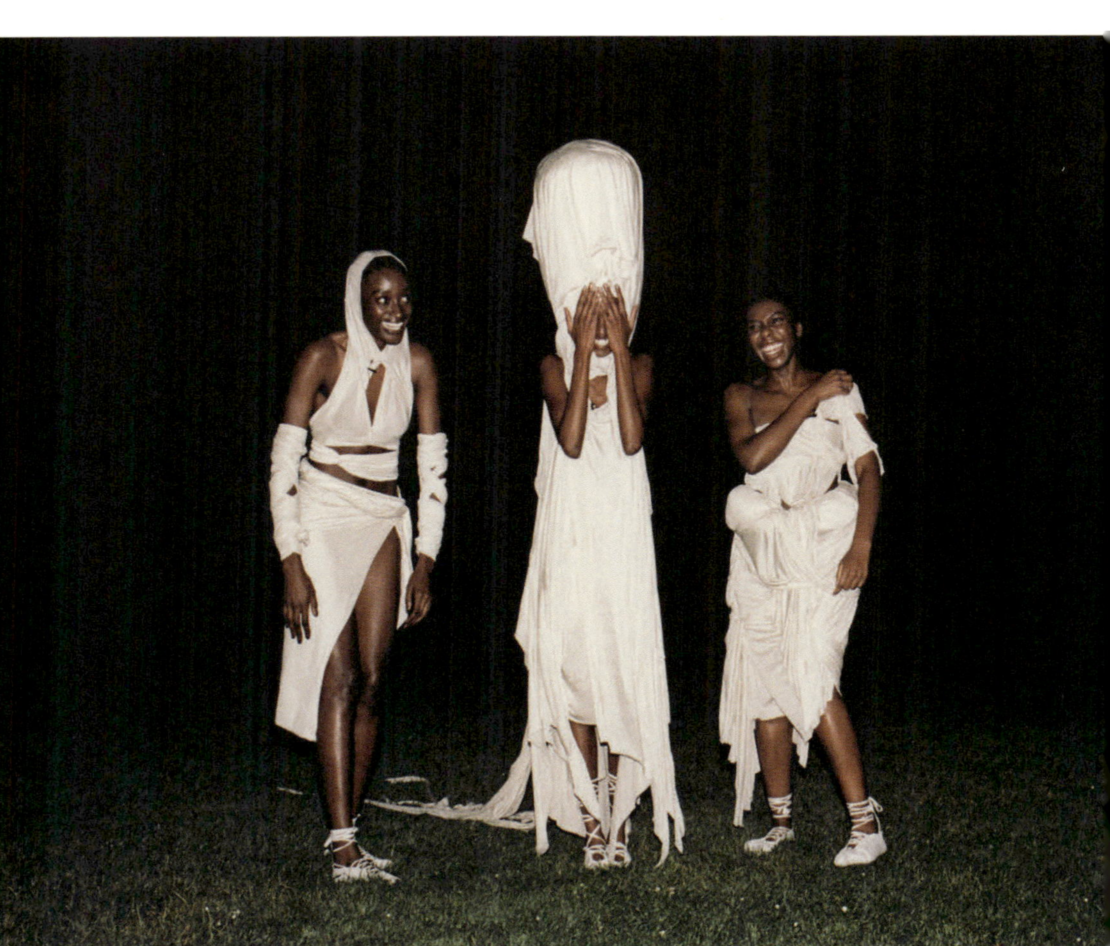

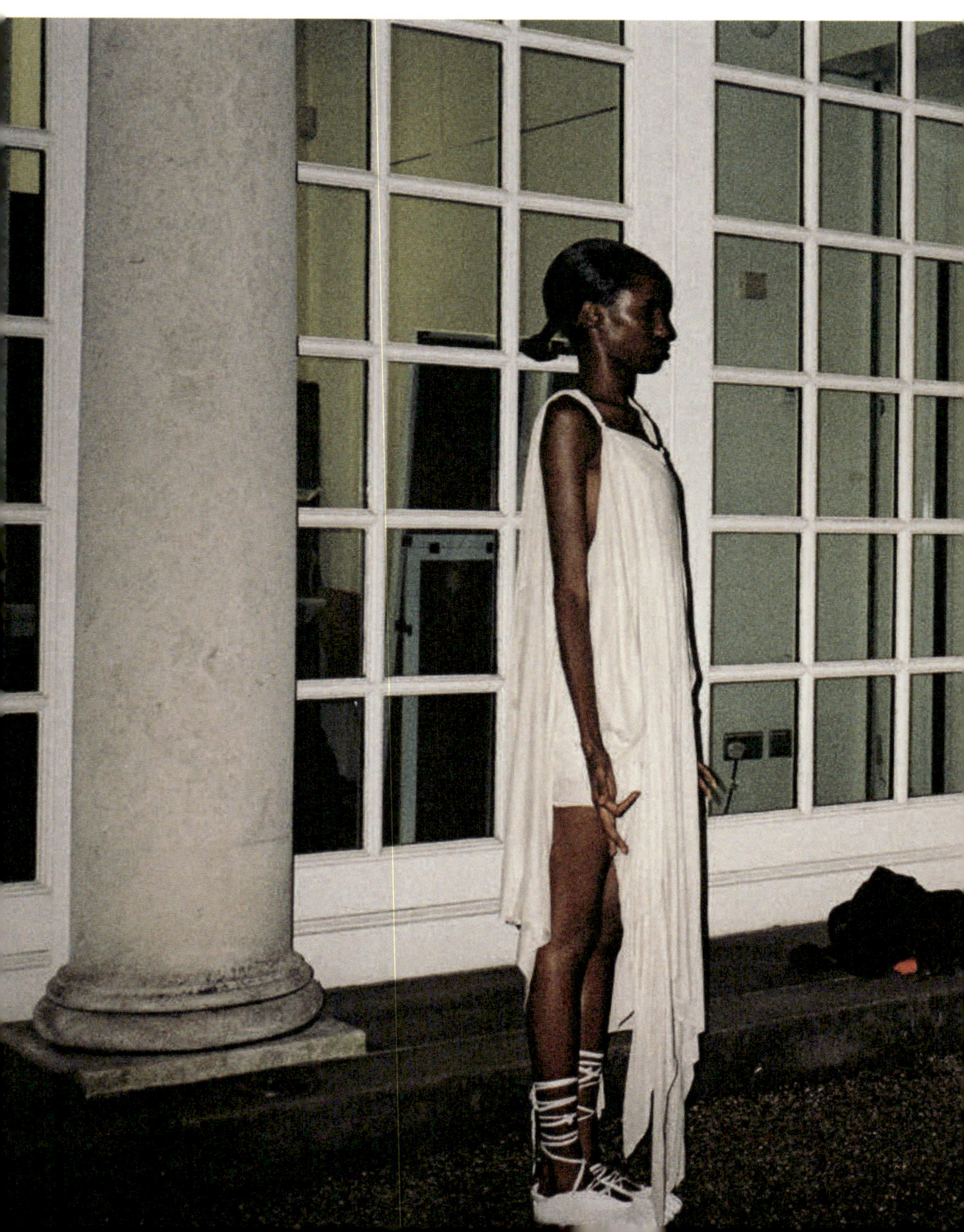

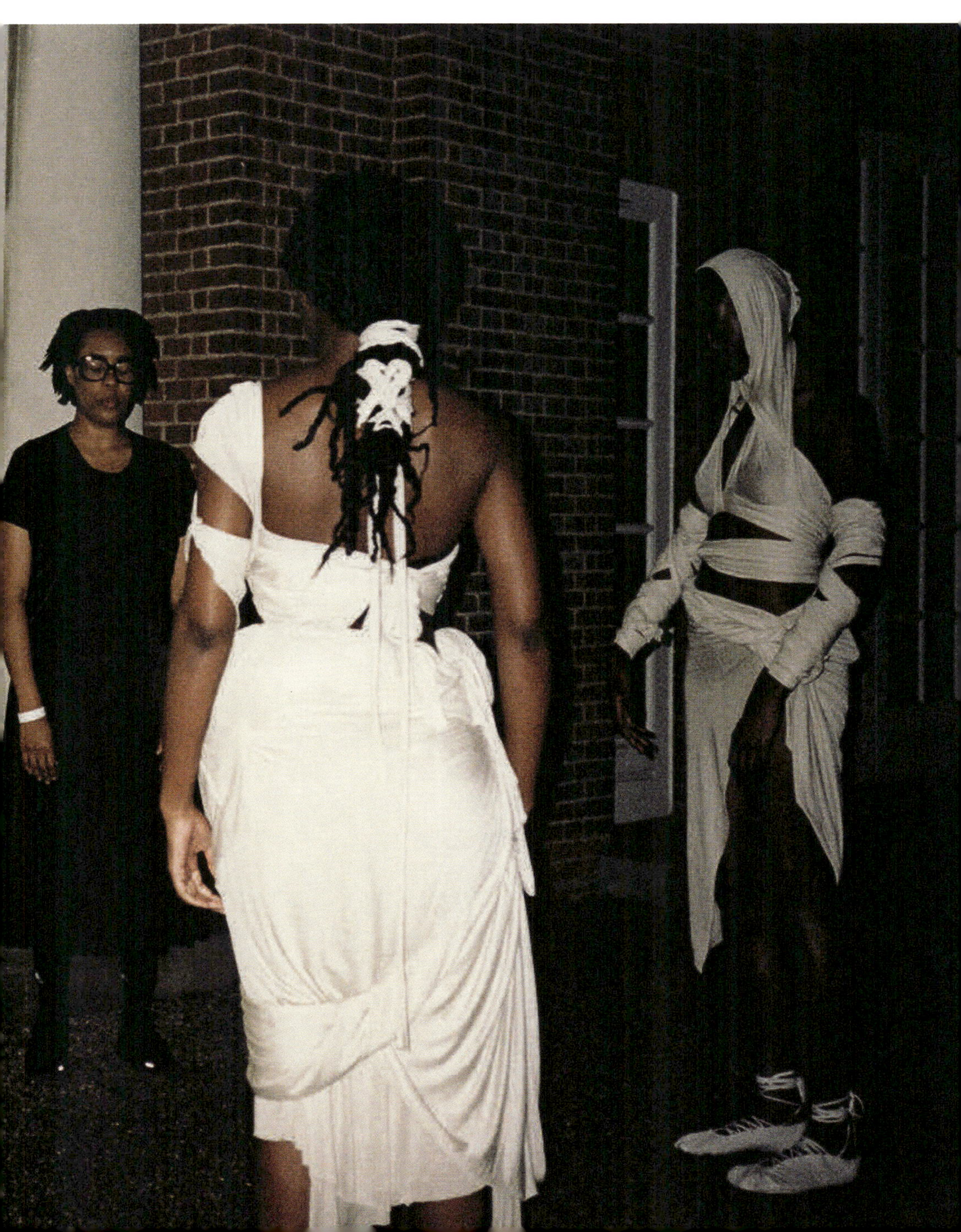

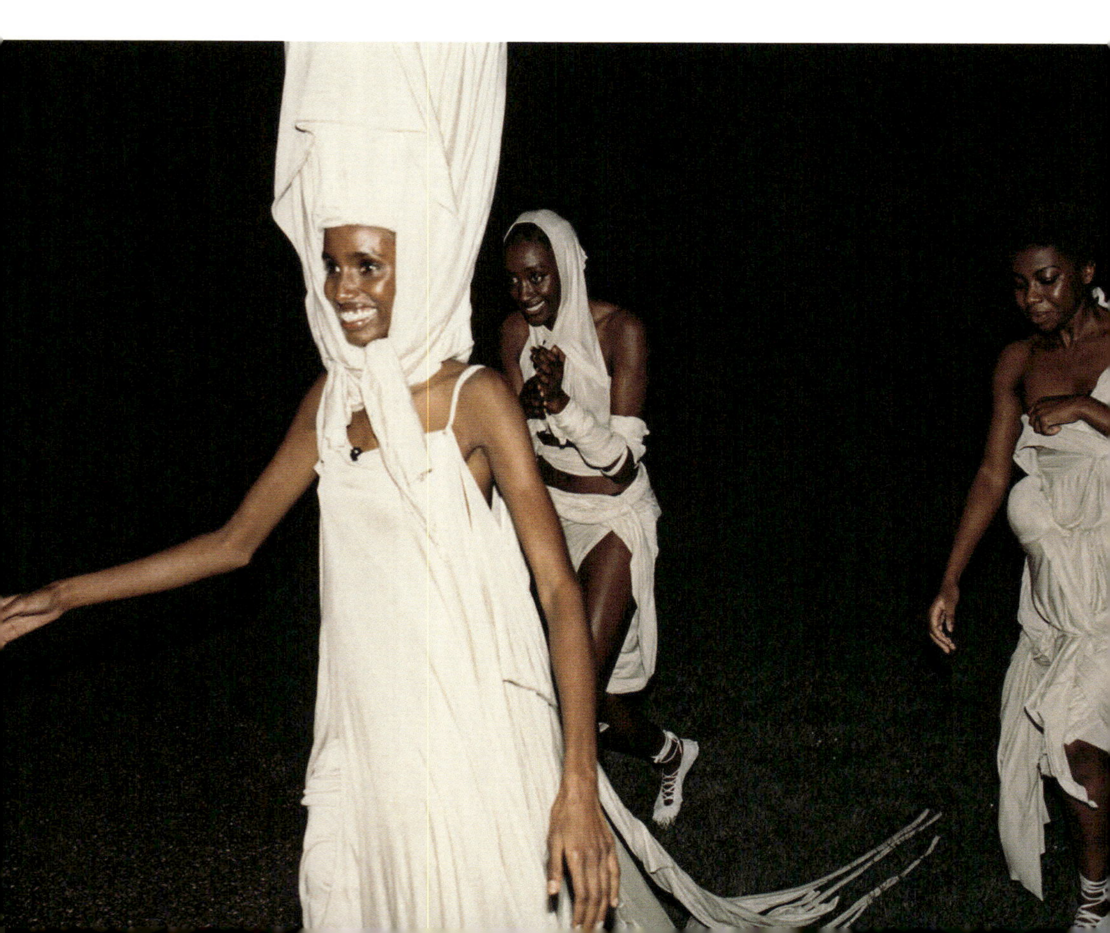

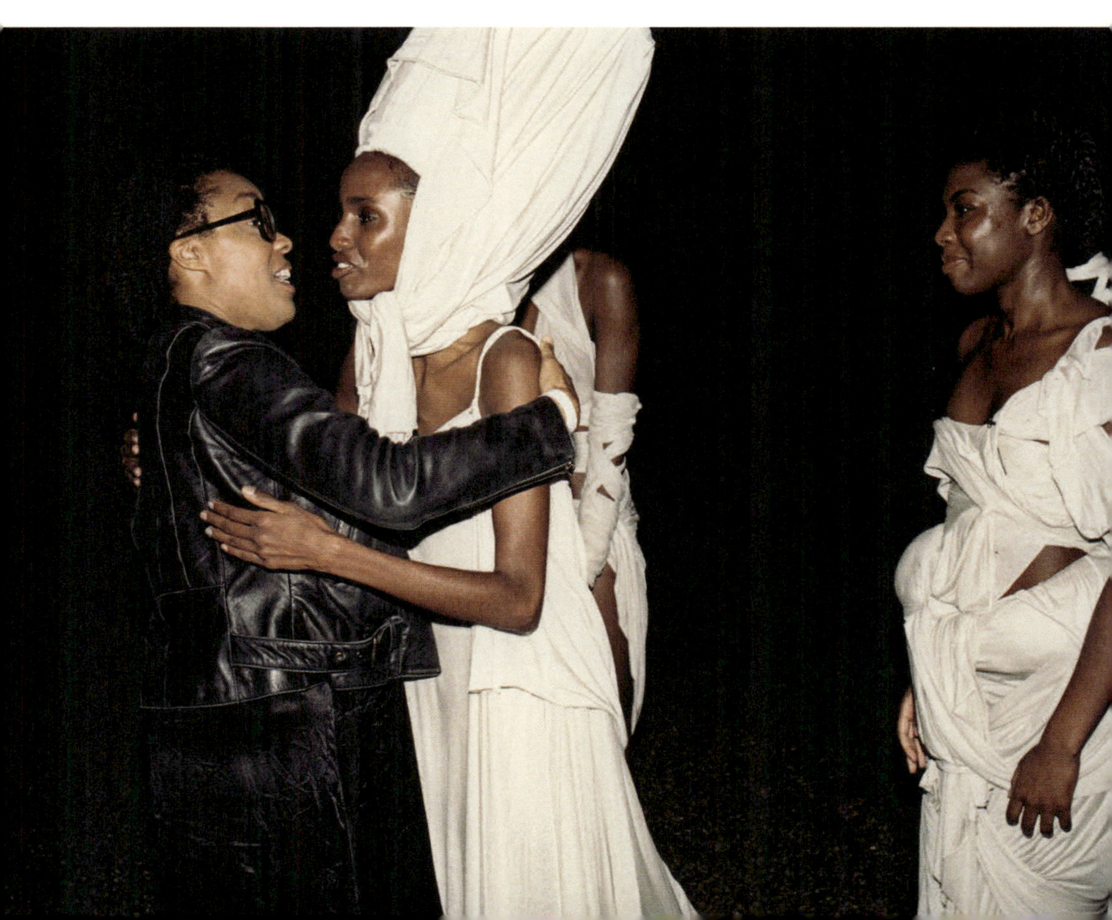

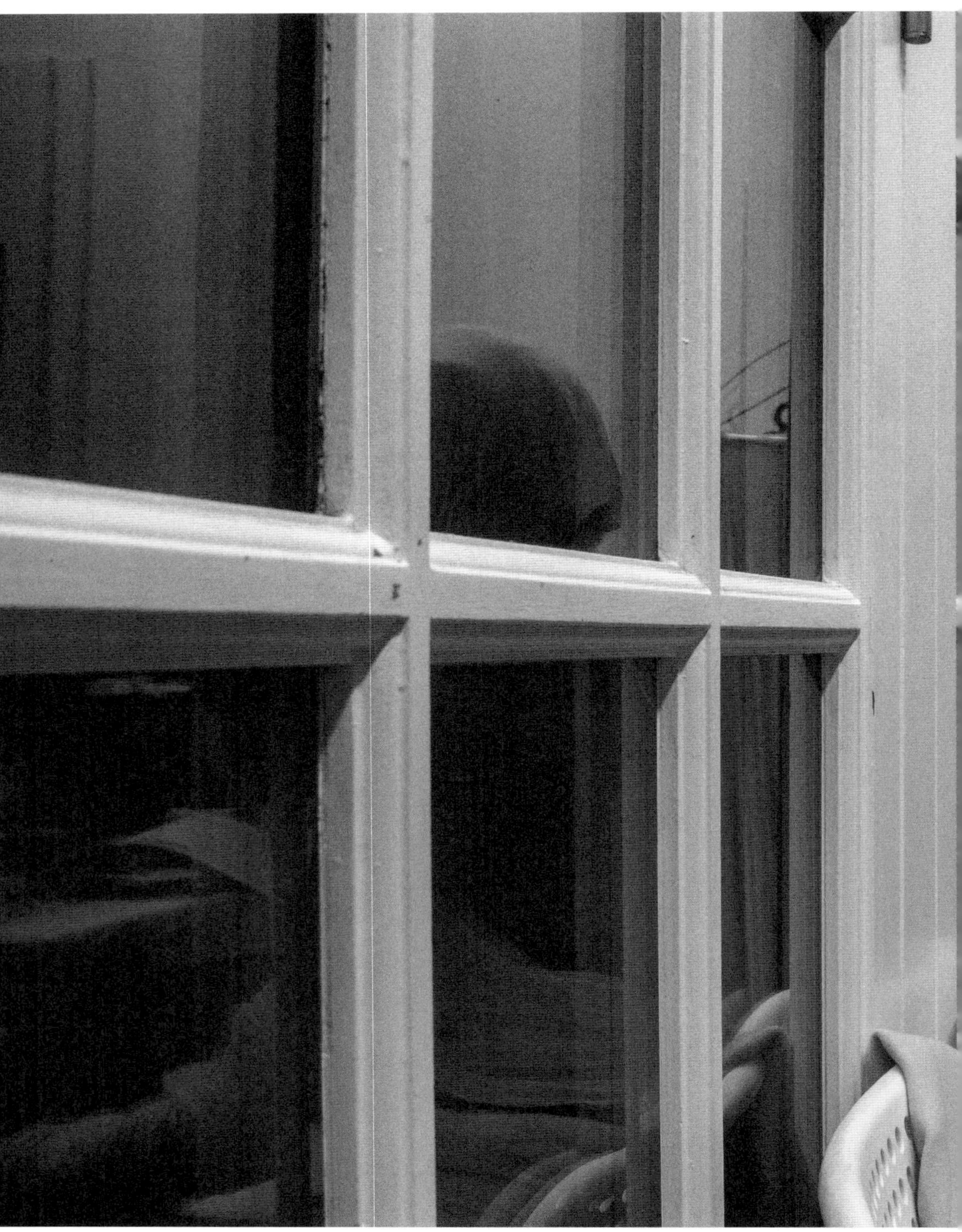

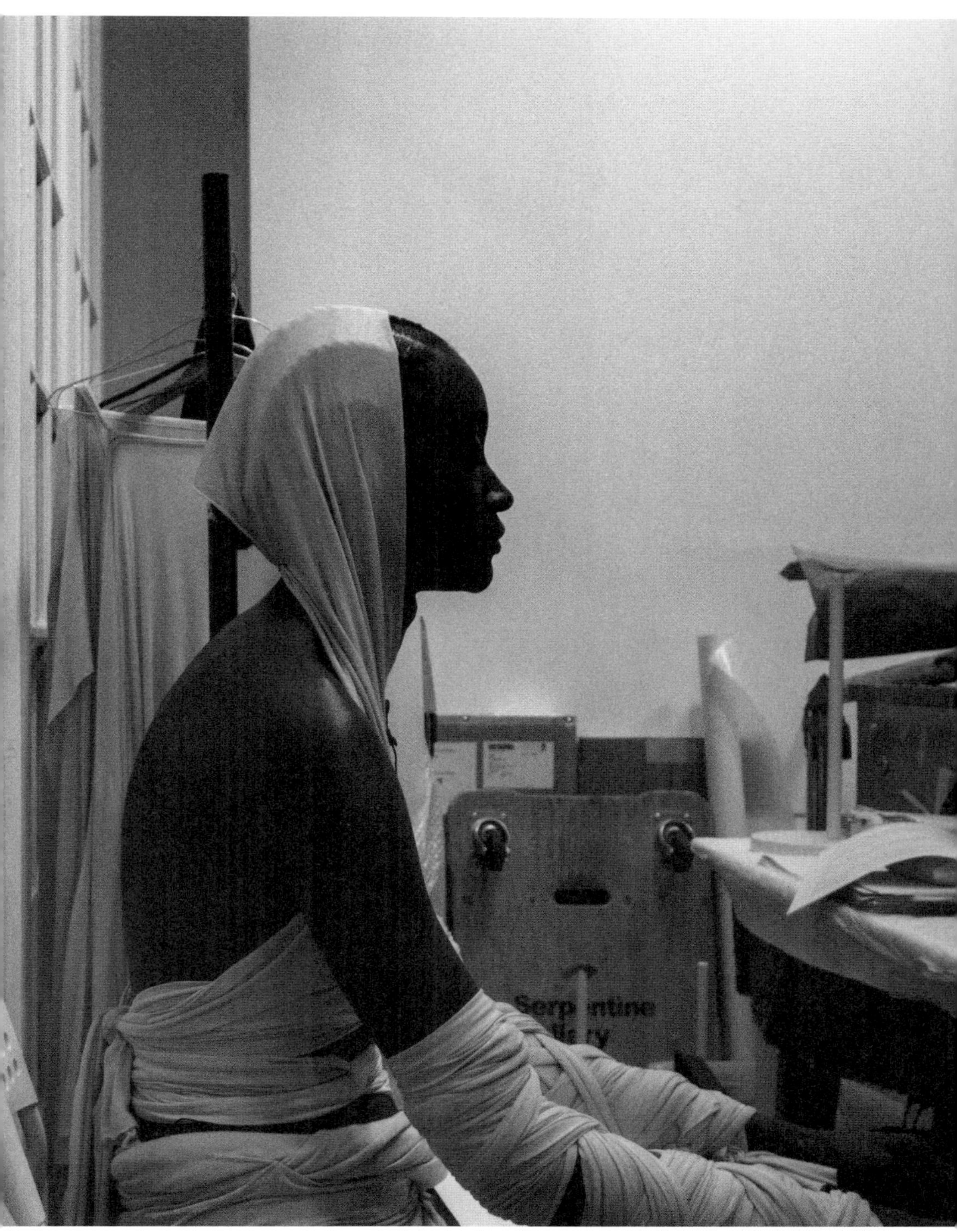
Serpentine

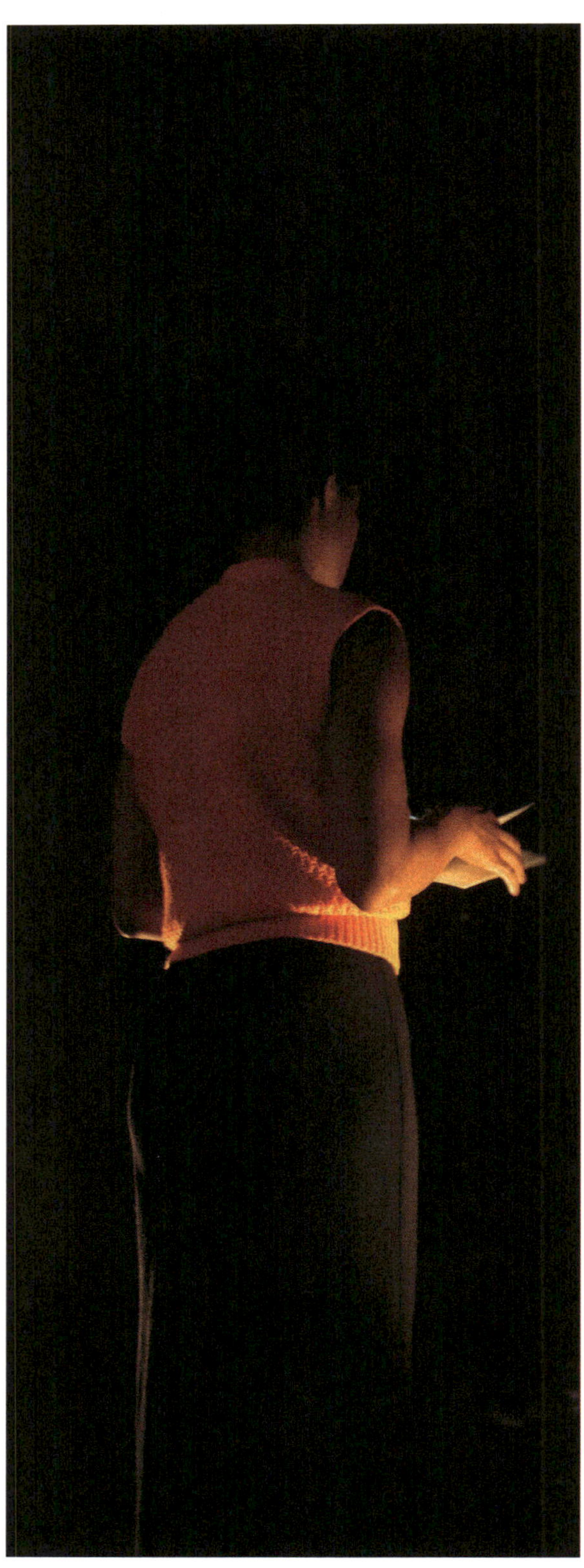

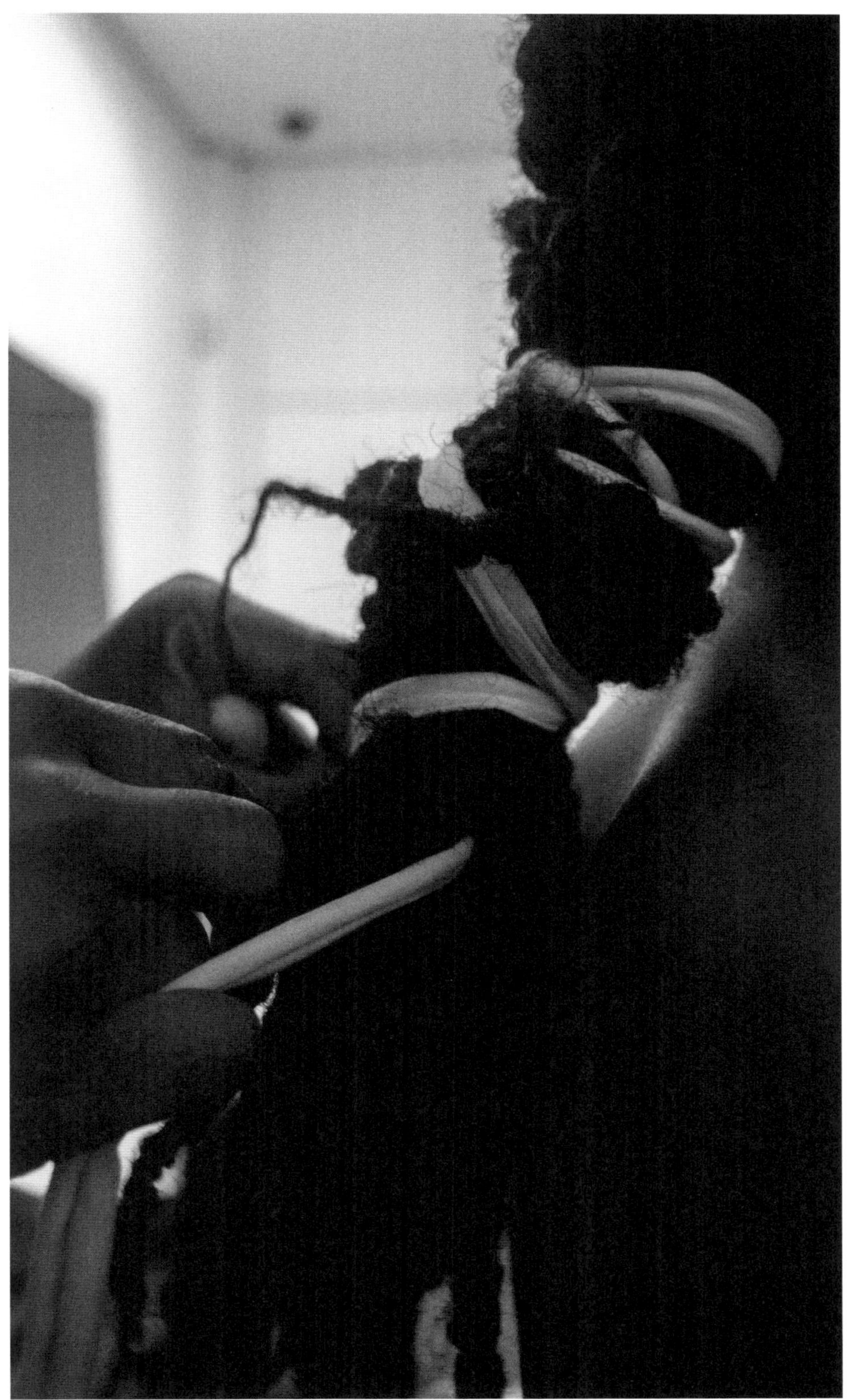

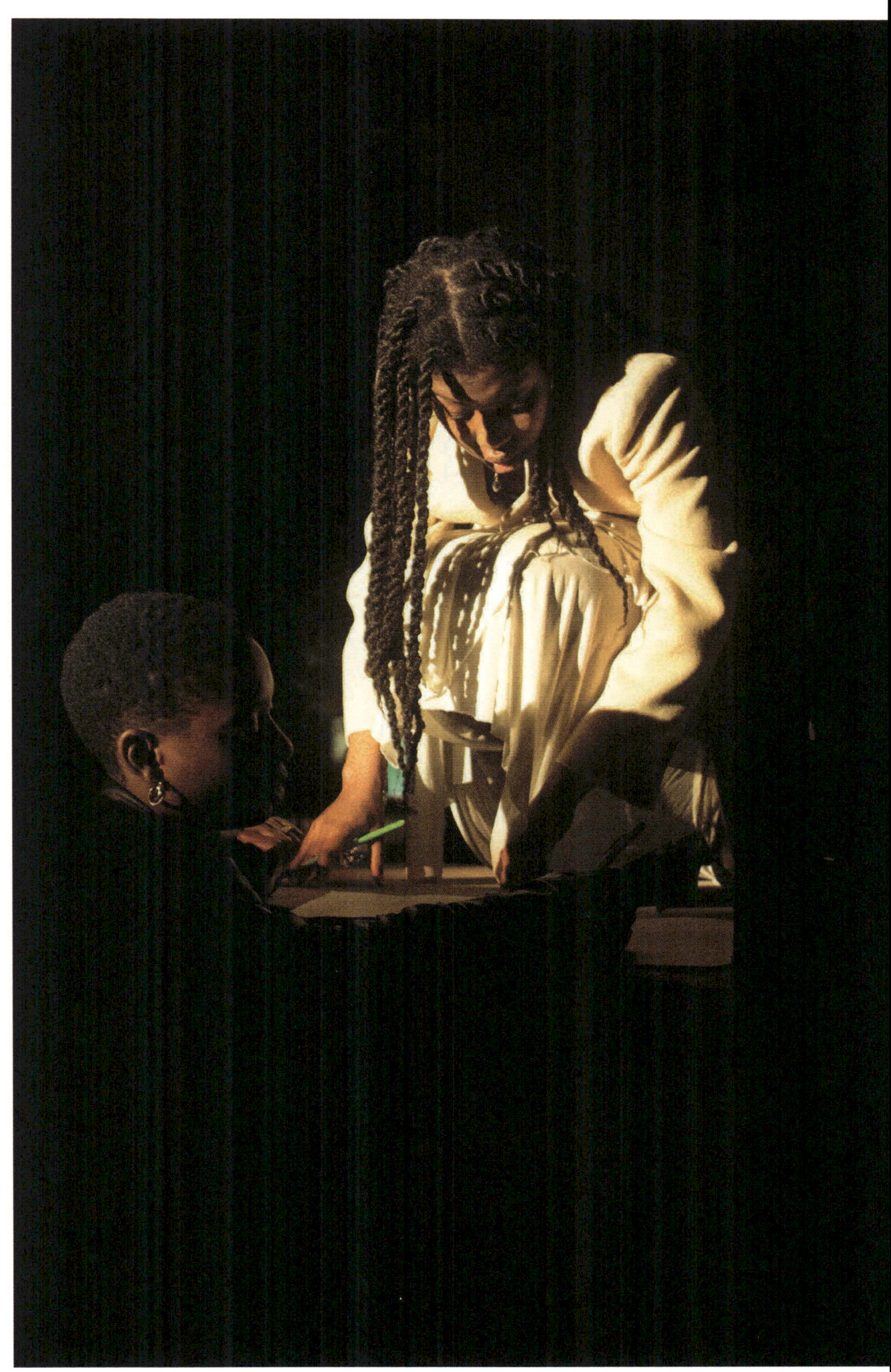

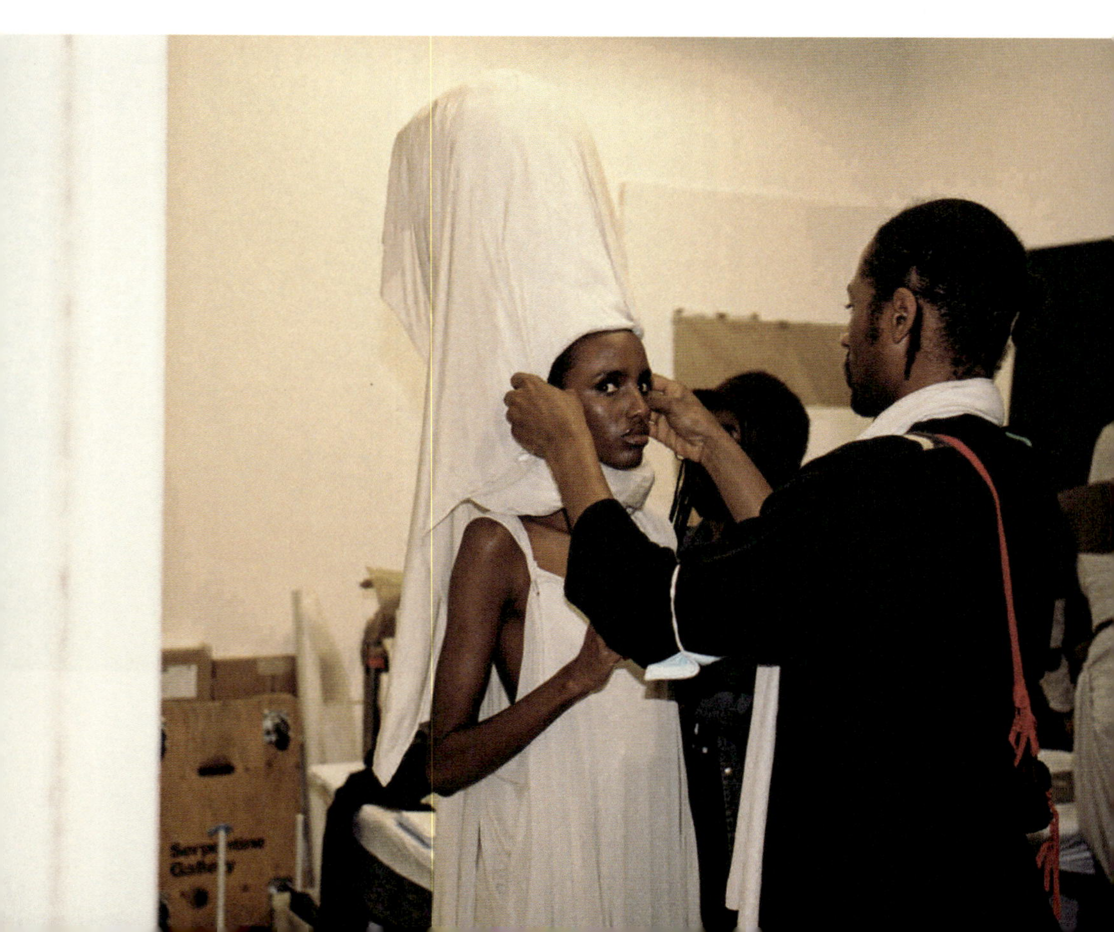

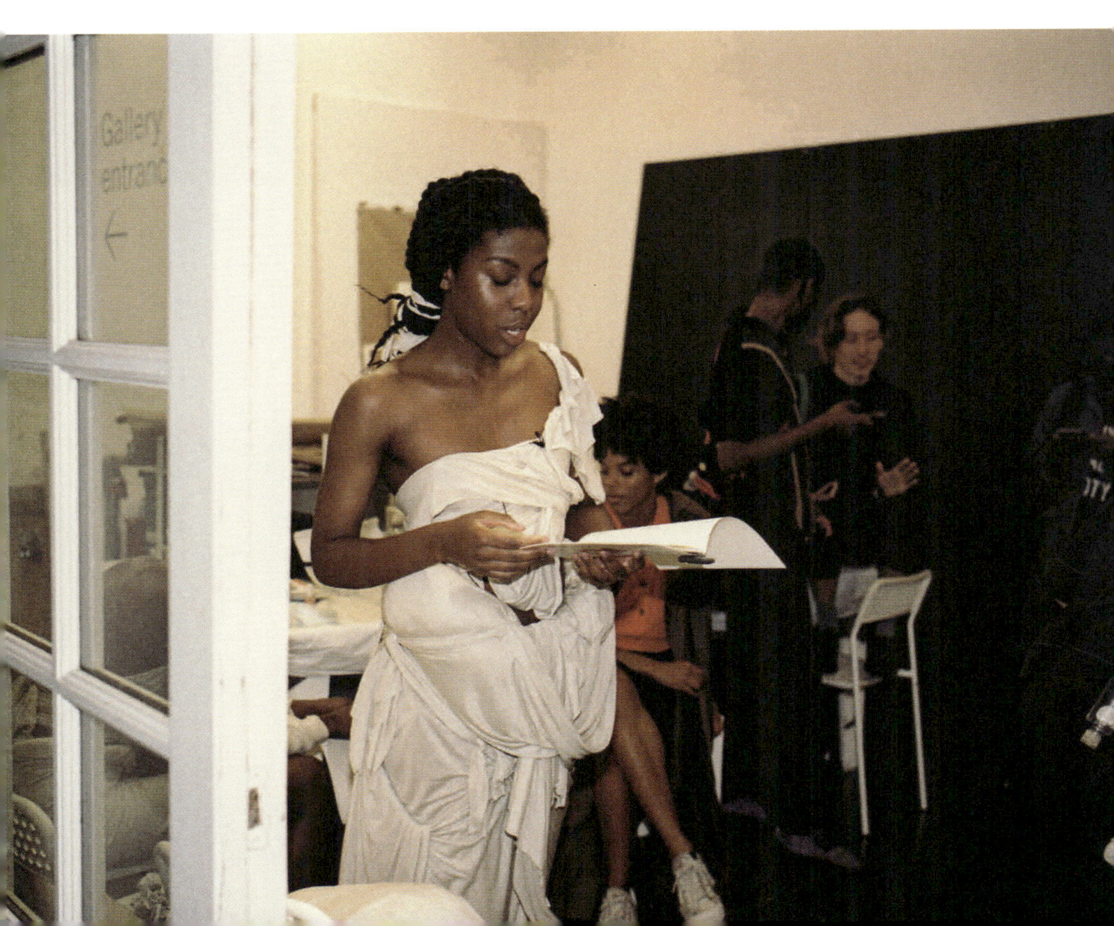
Gallery

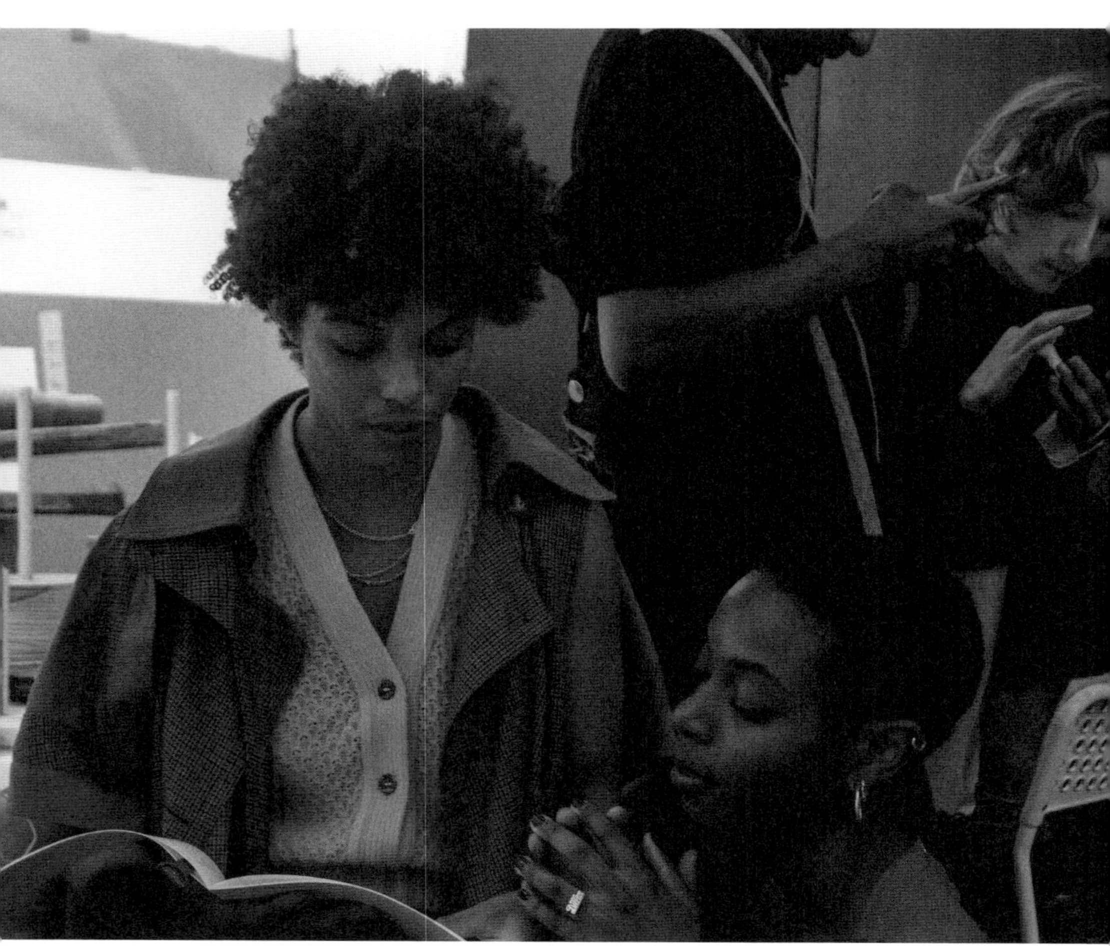

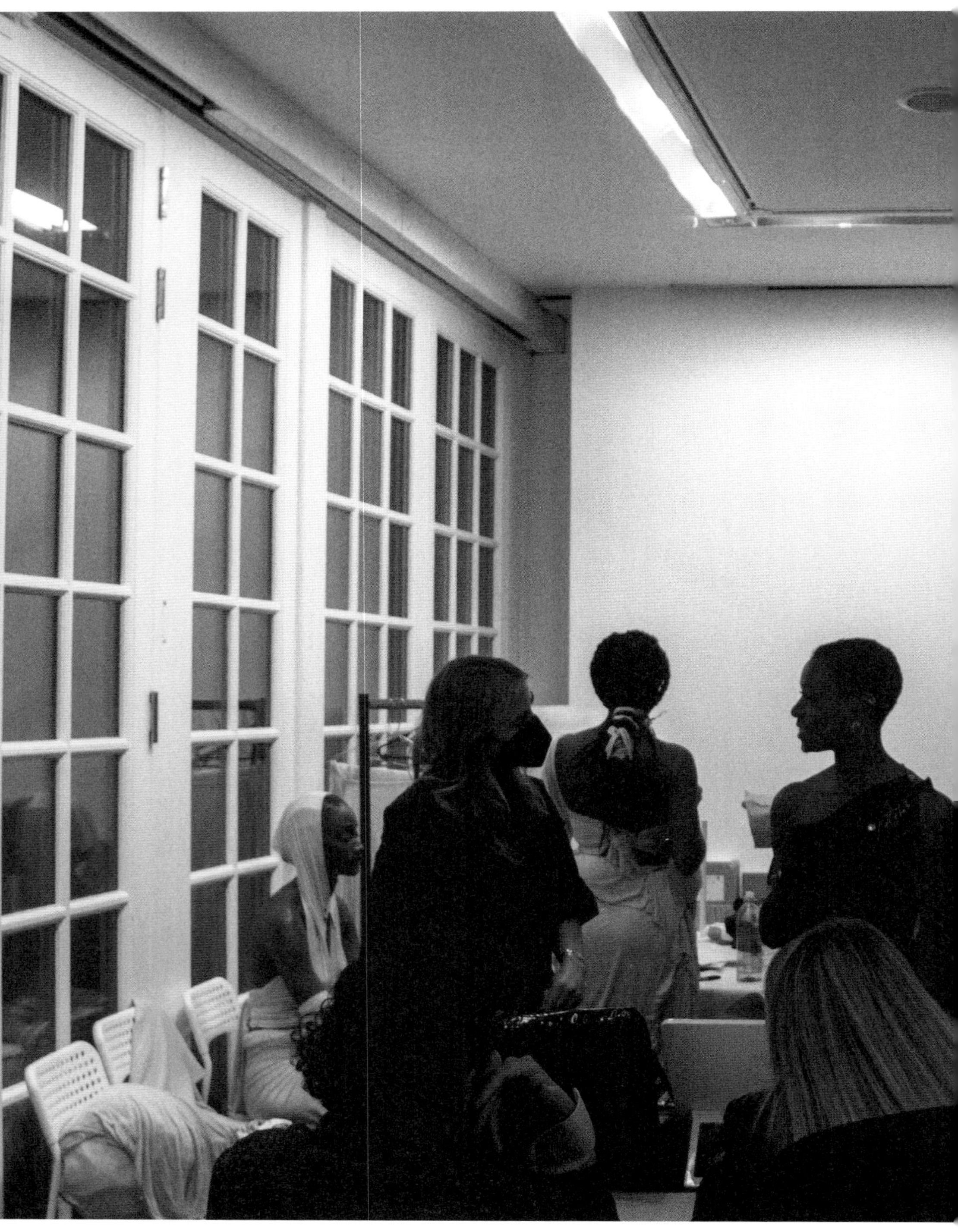

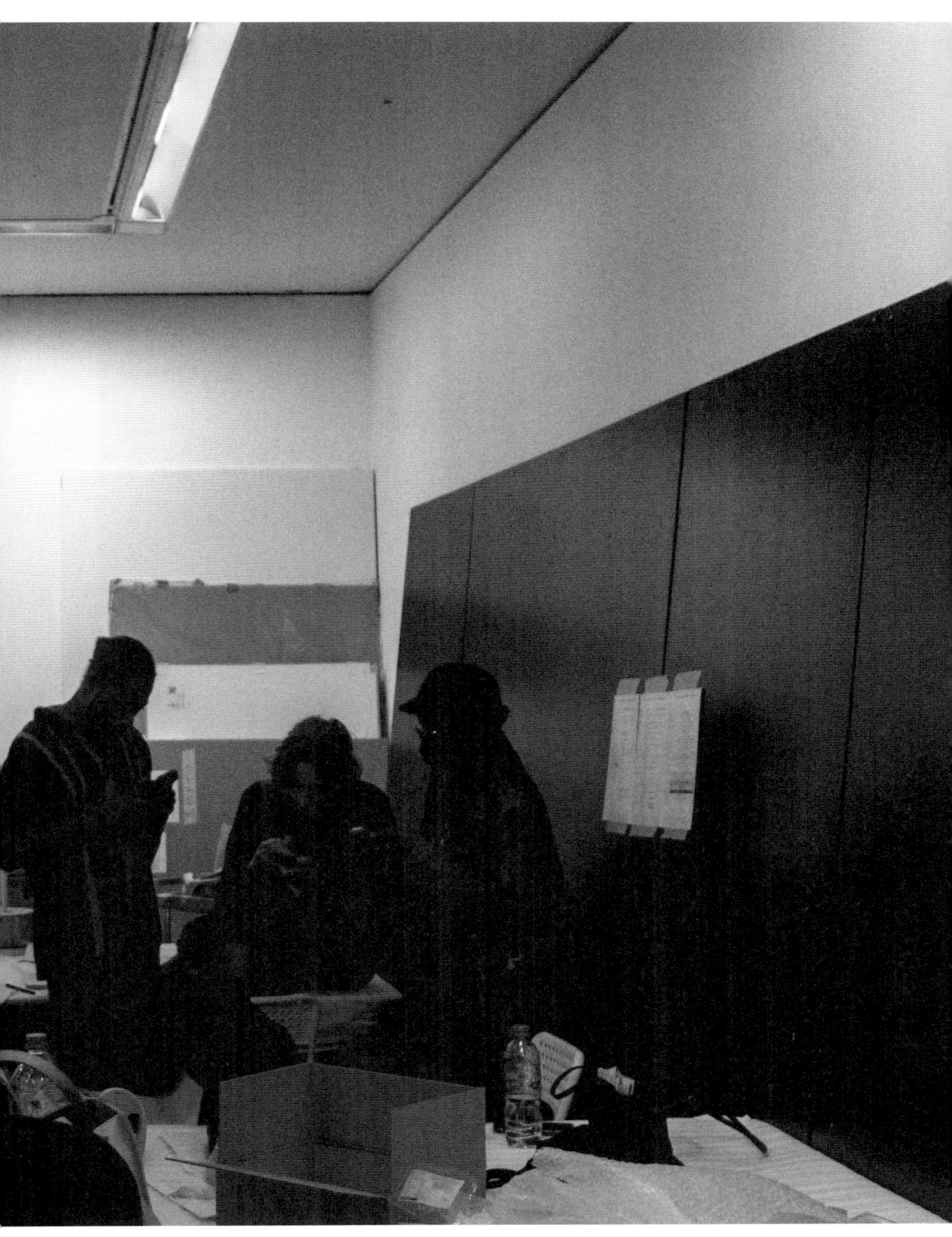

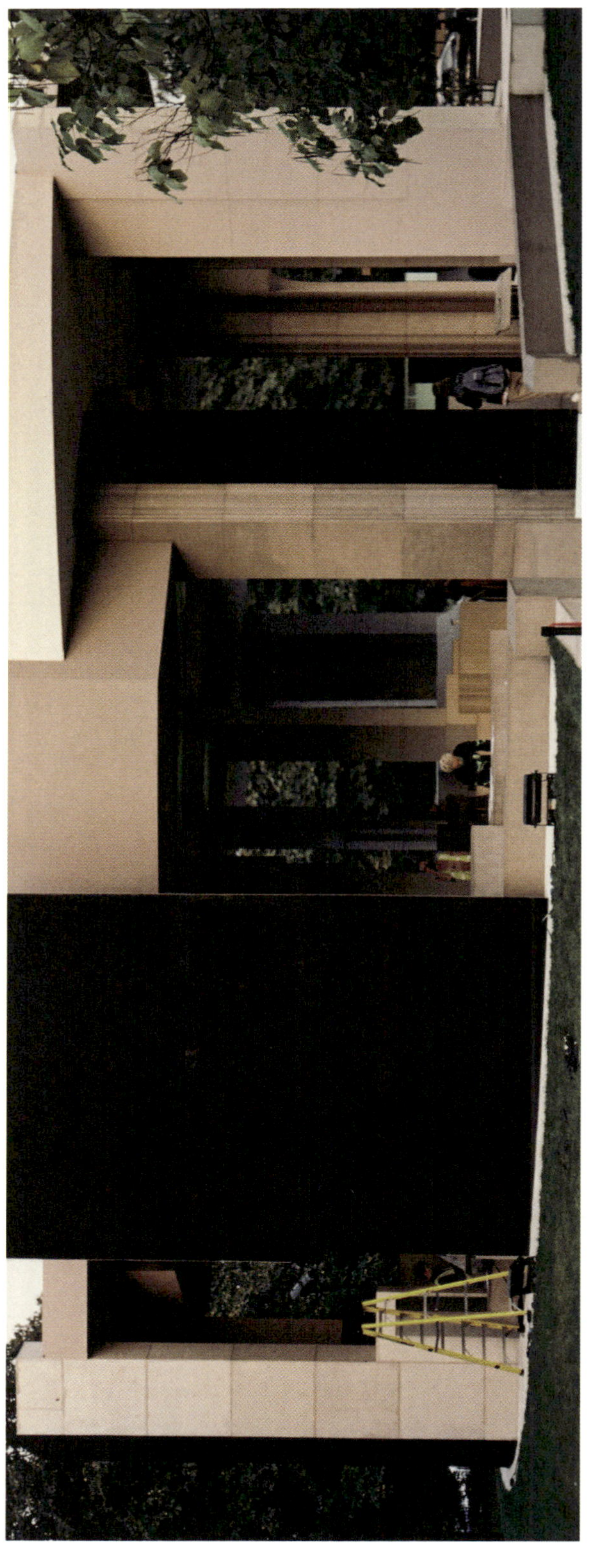

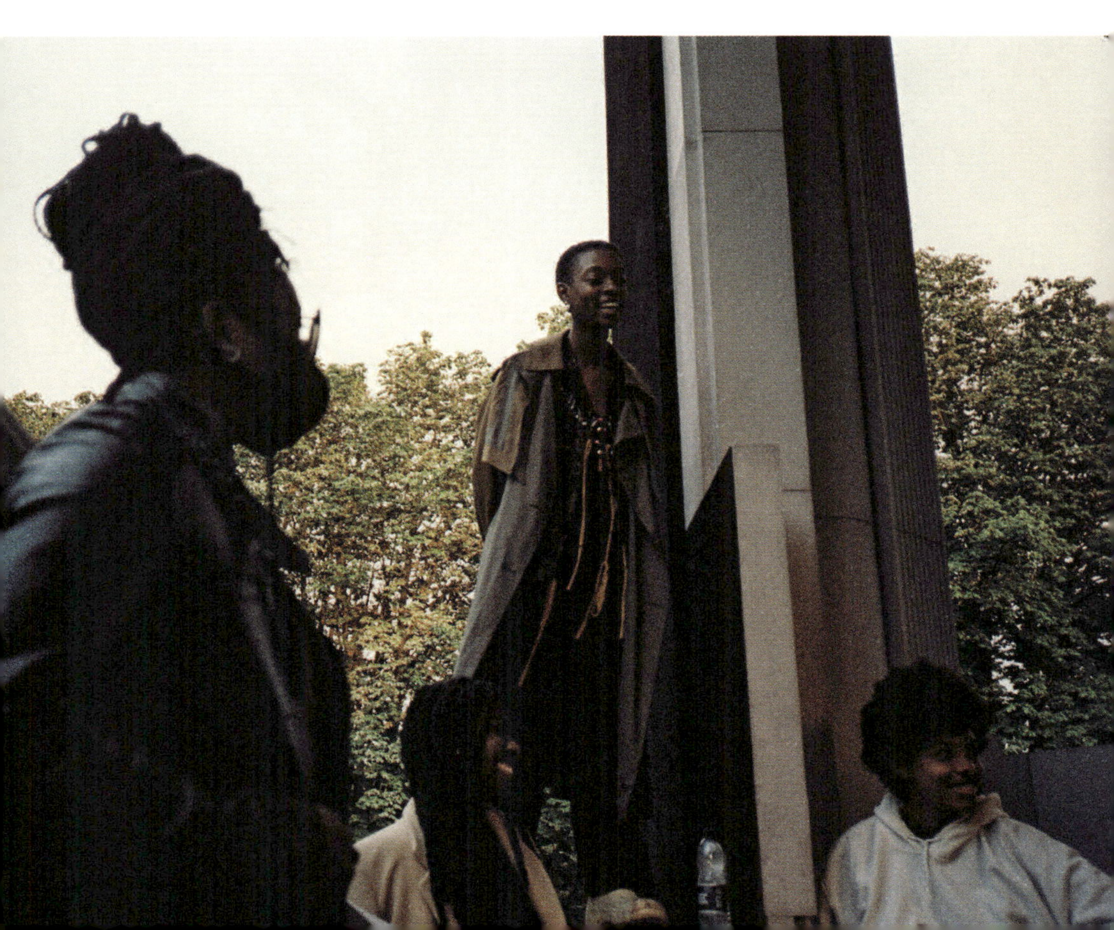

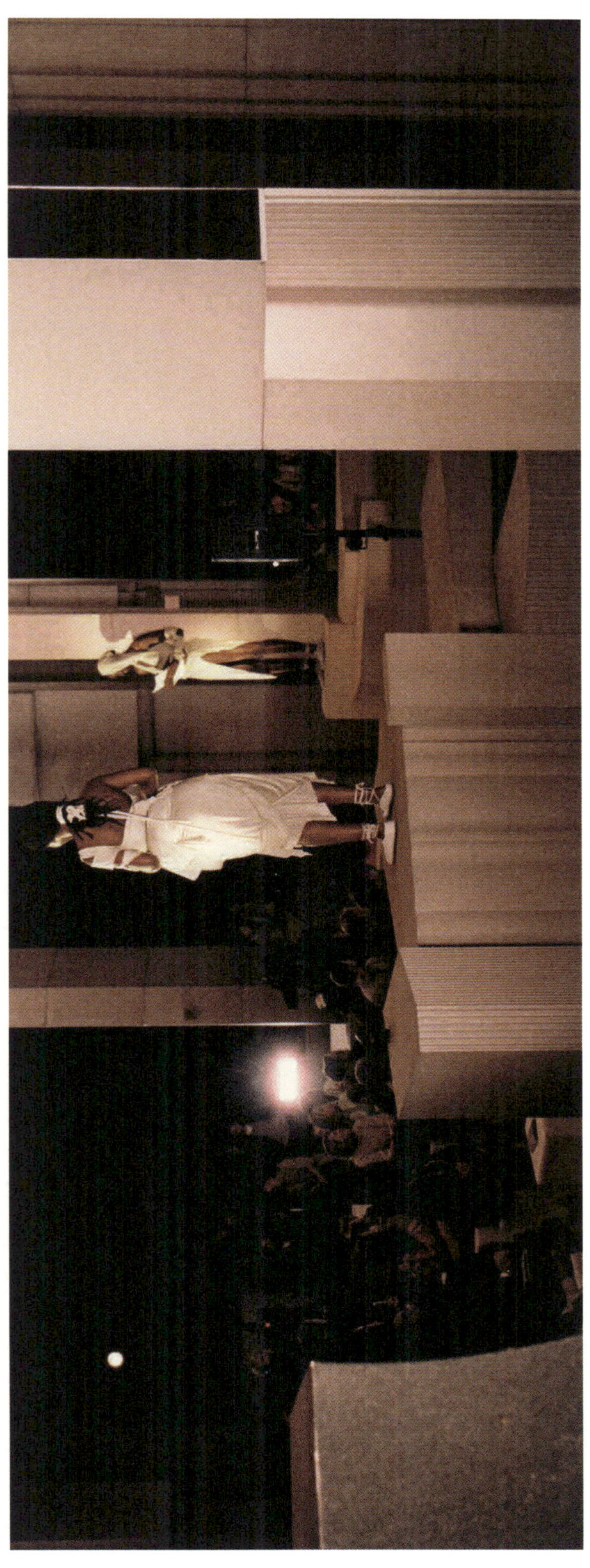

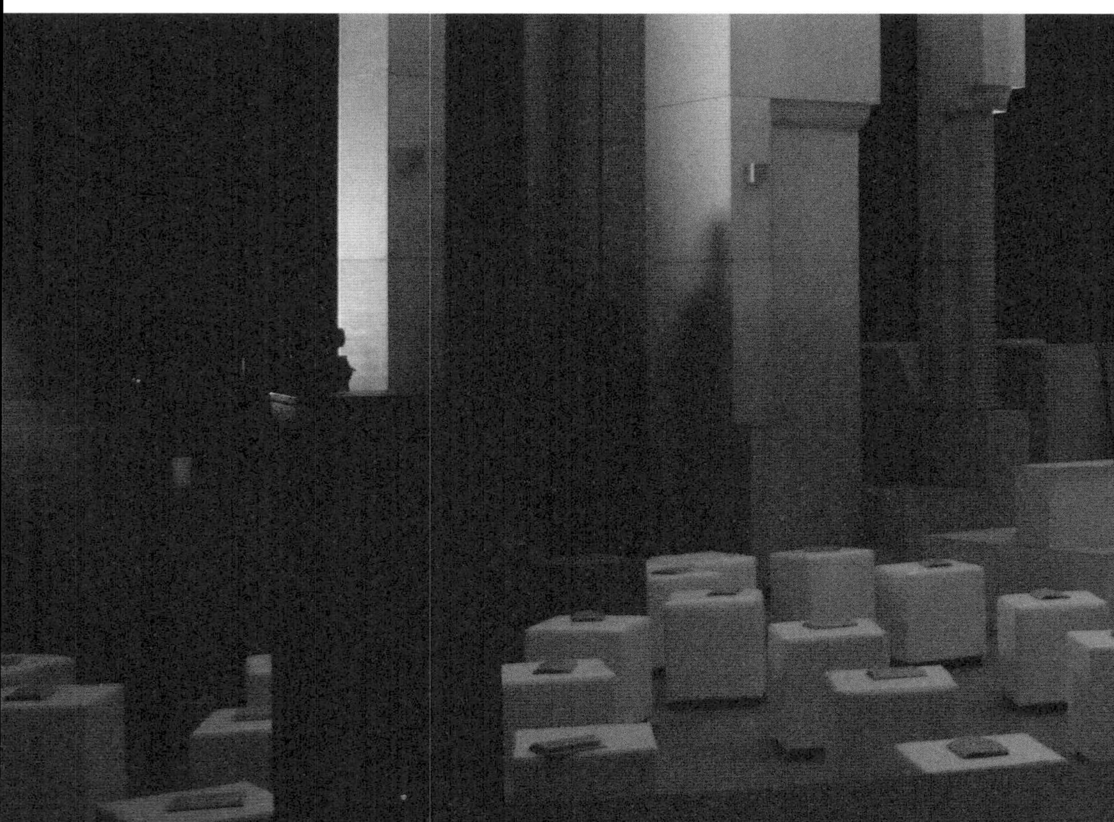

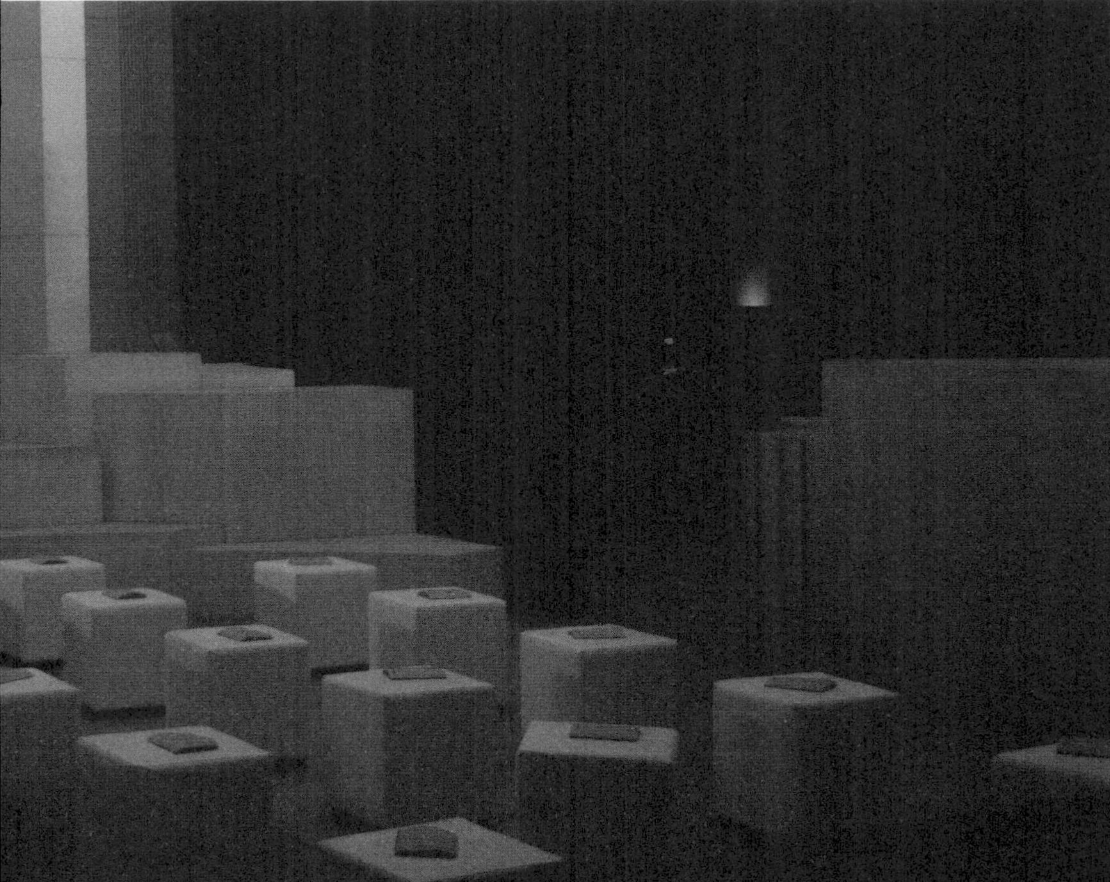

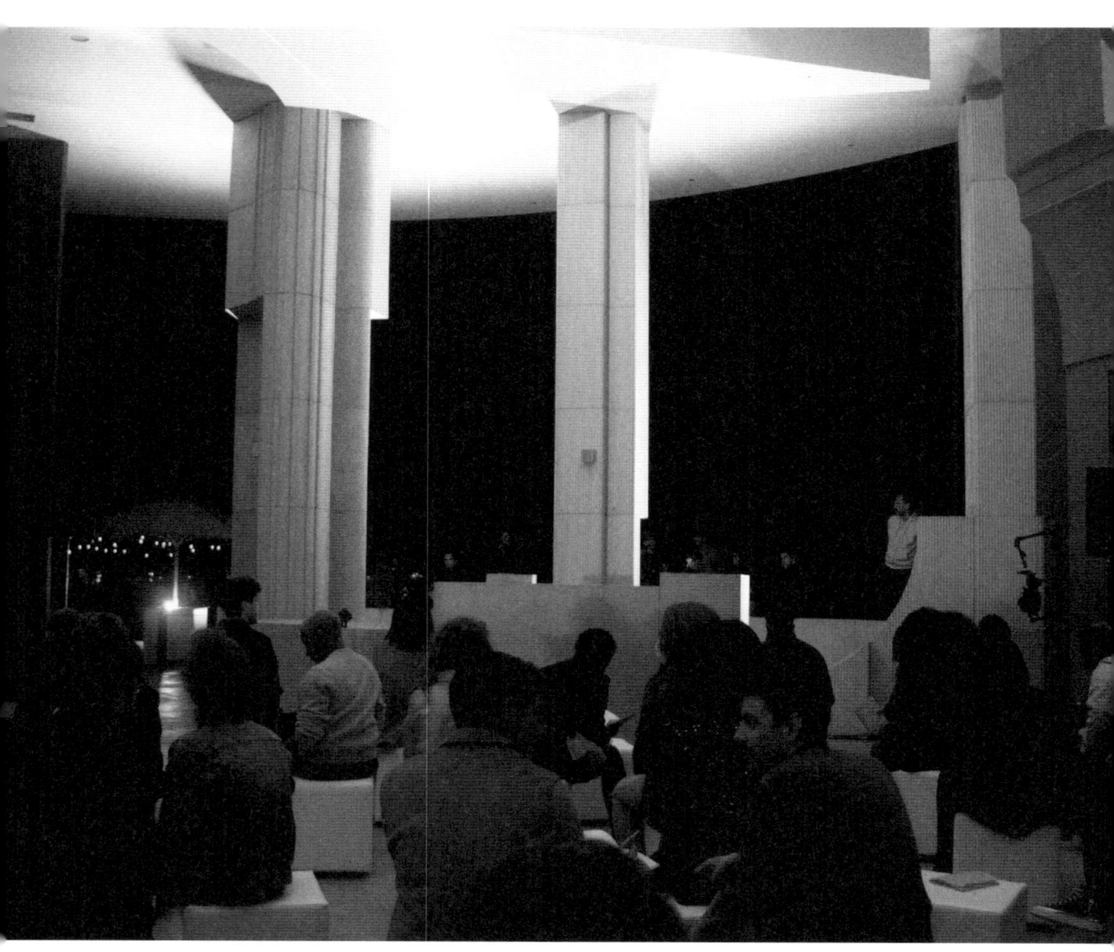

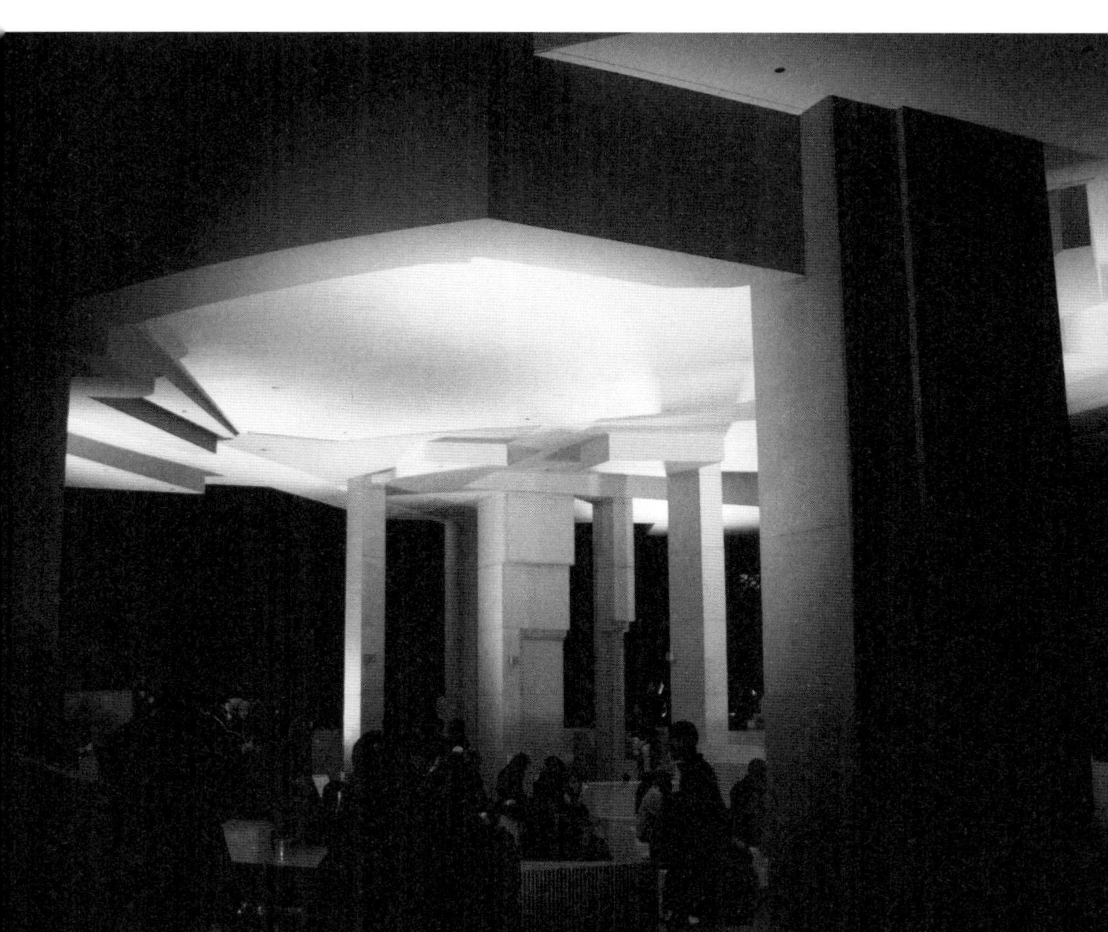

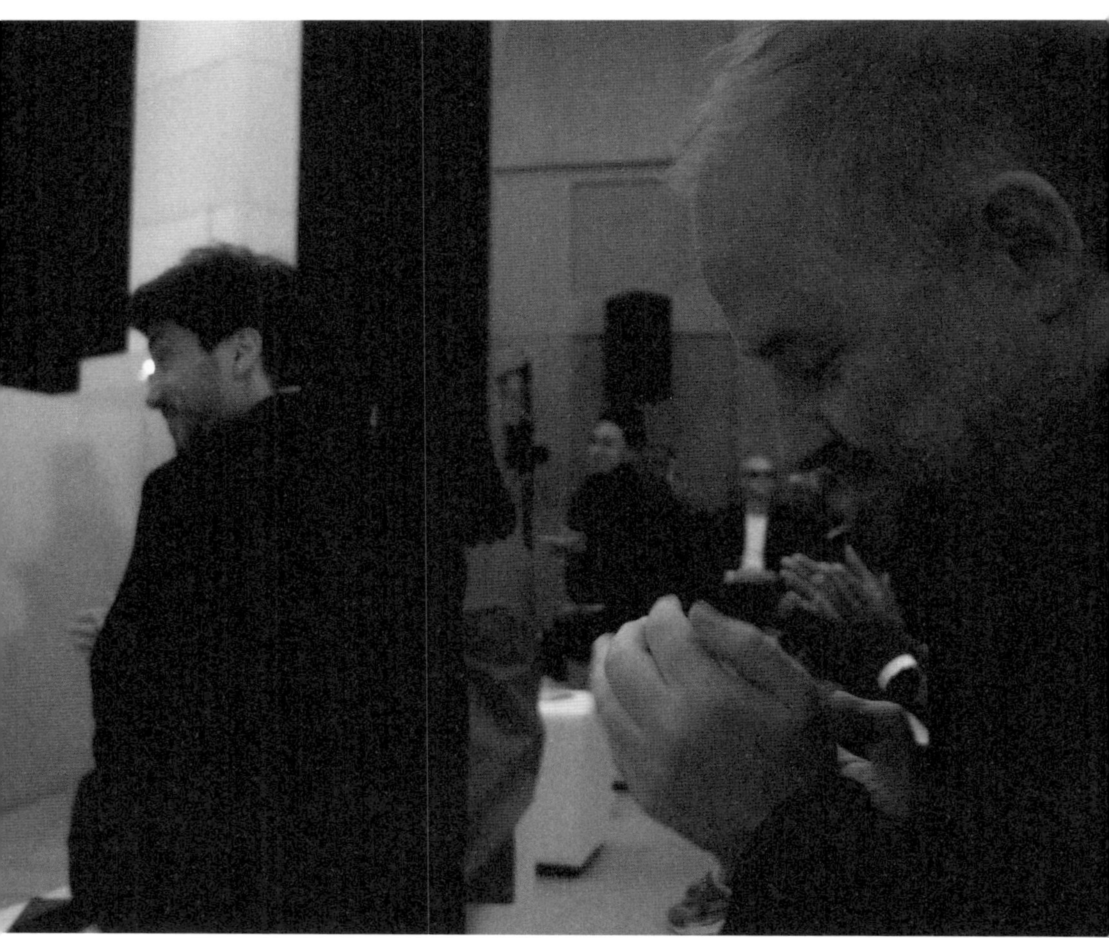

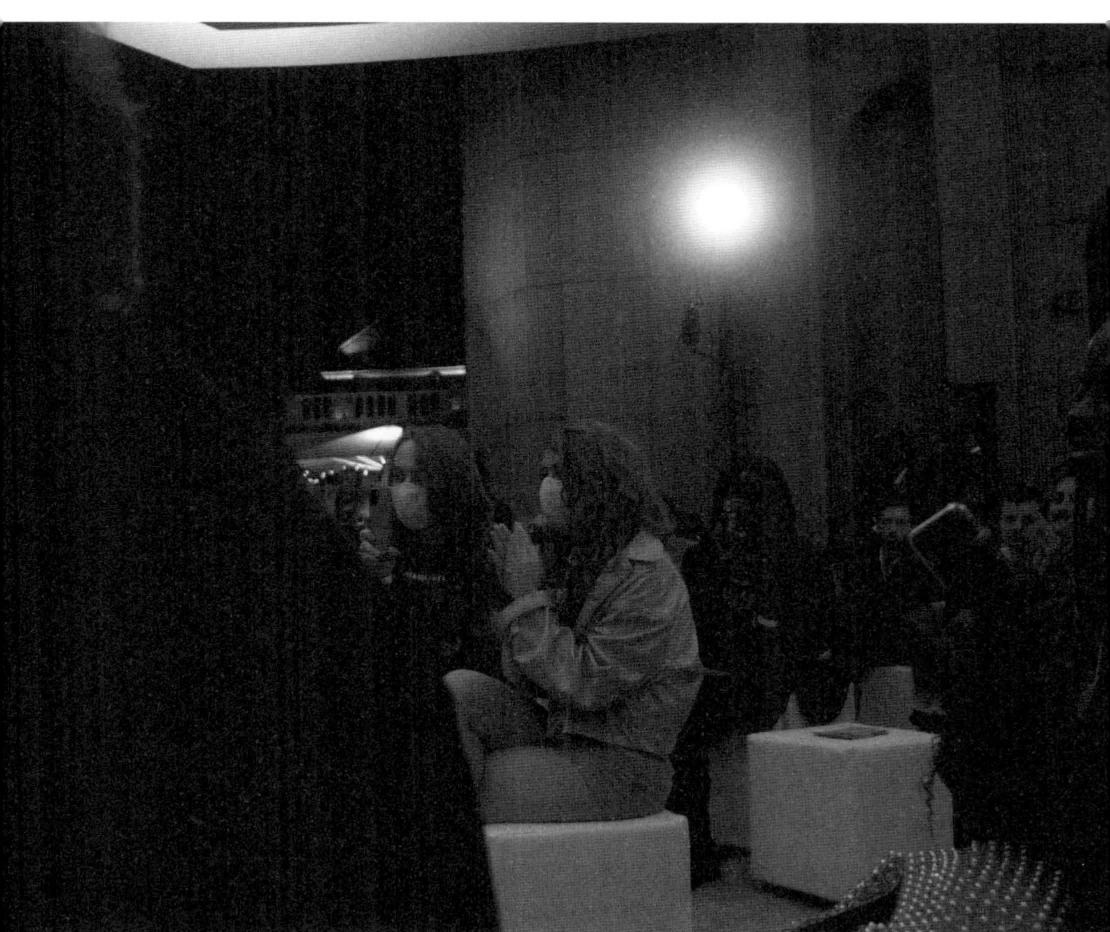

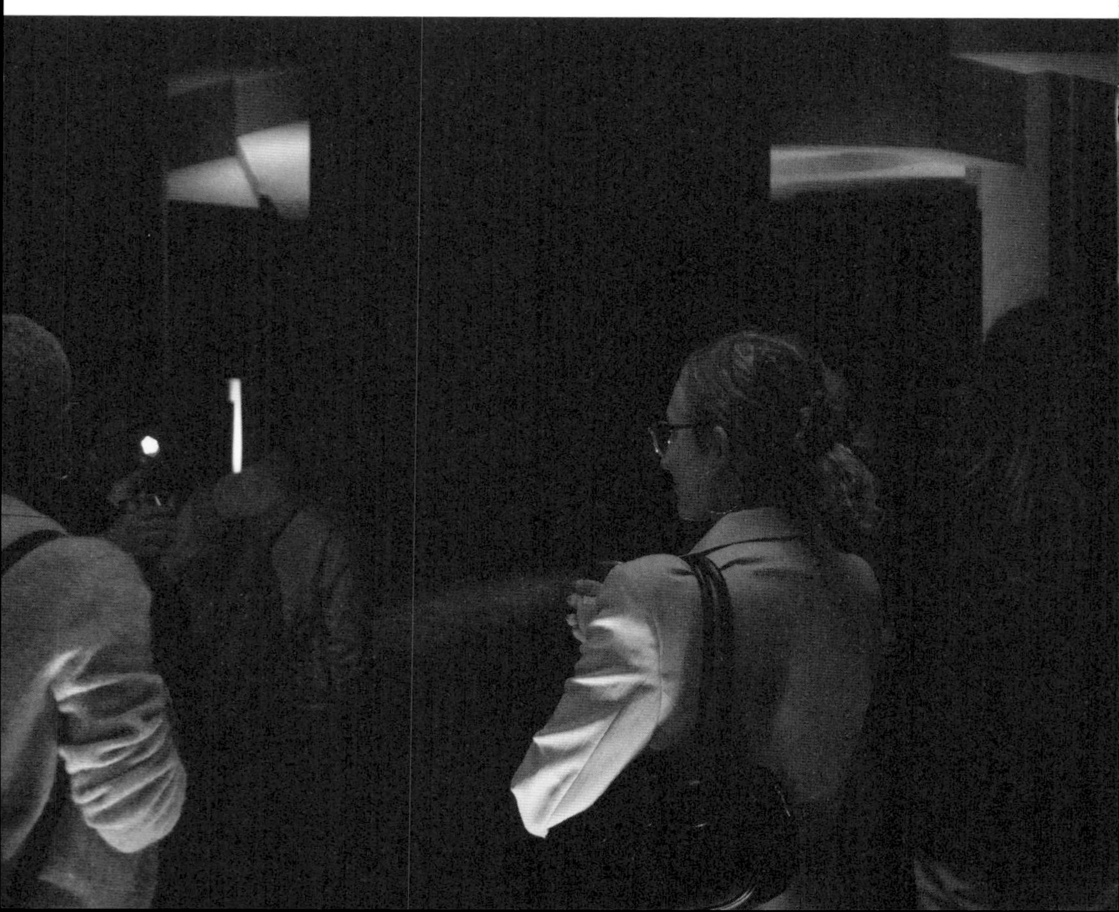

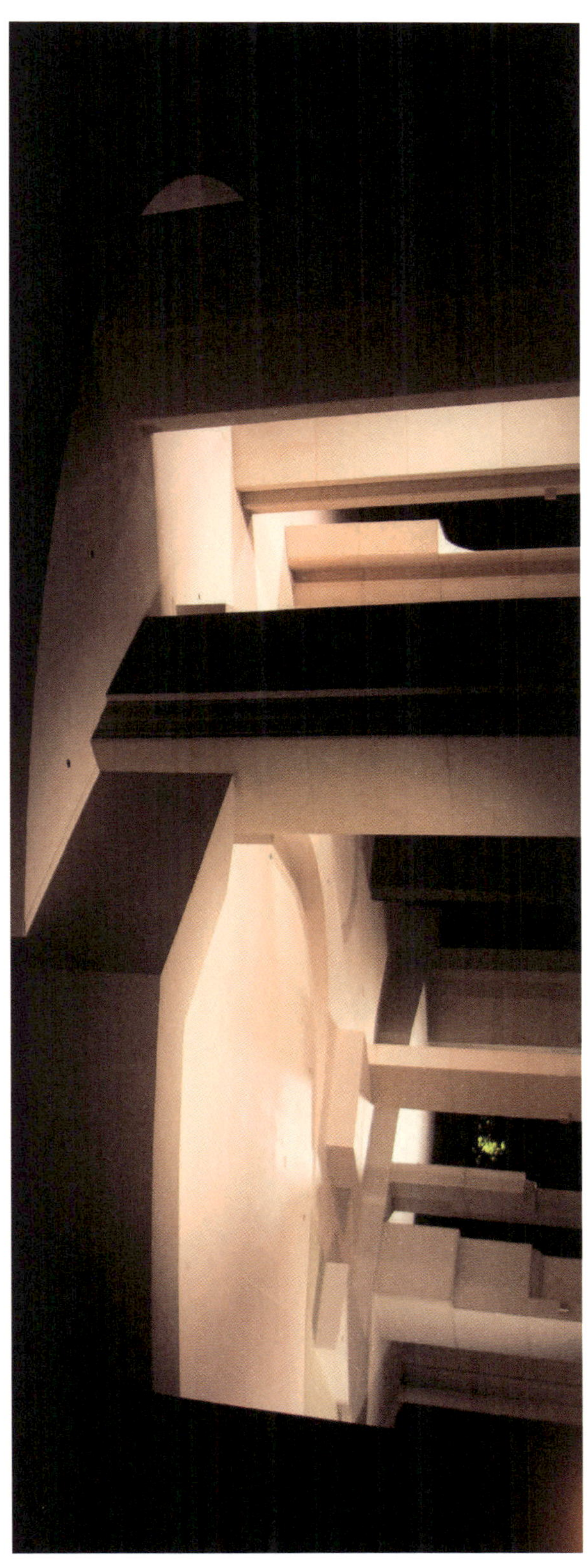

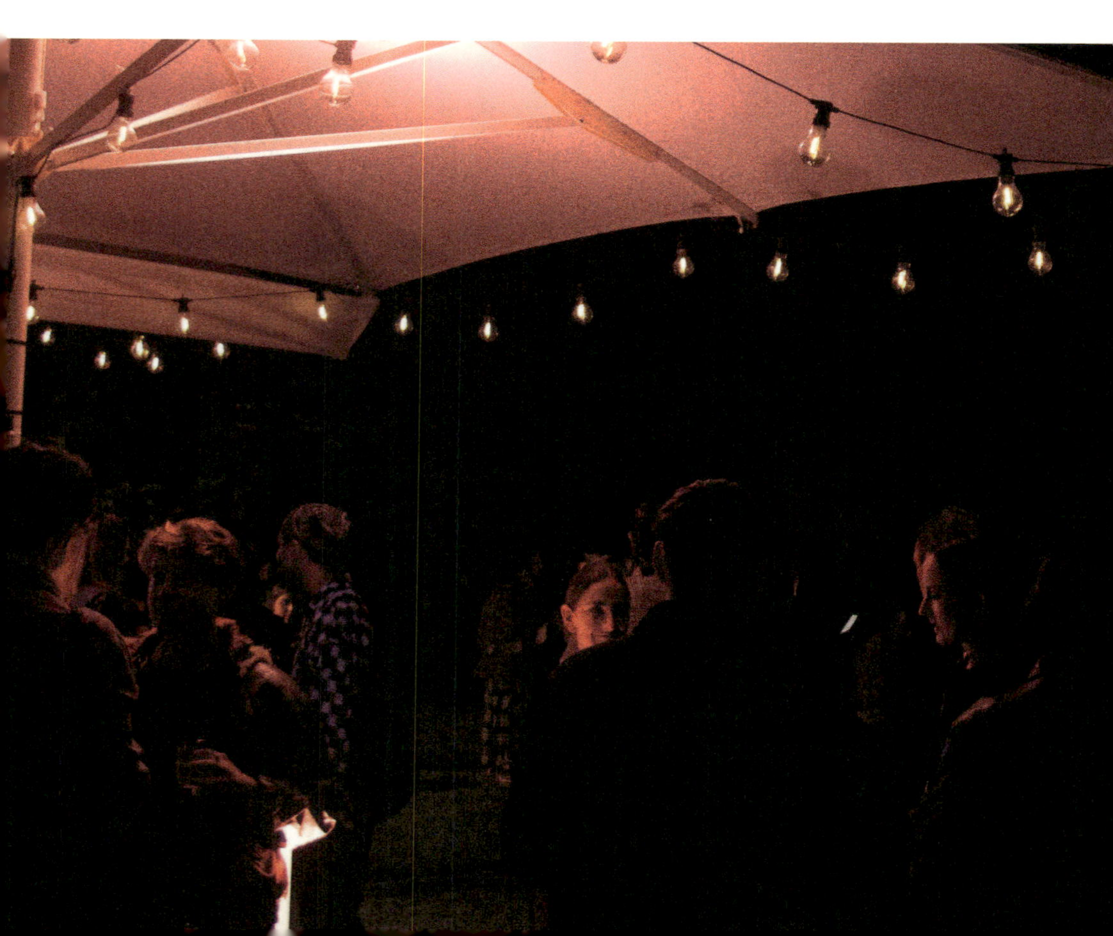

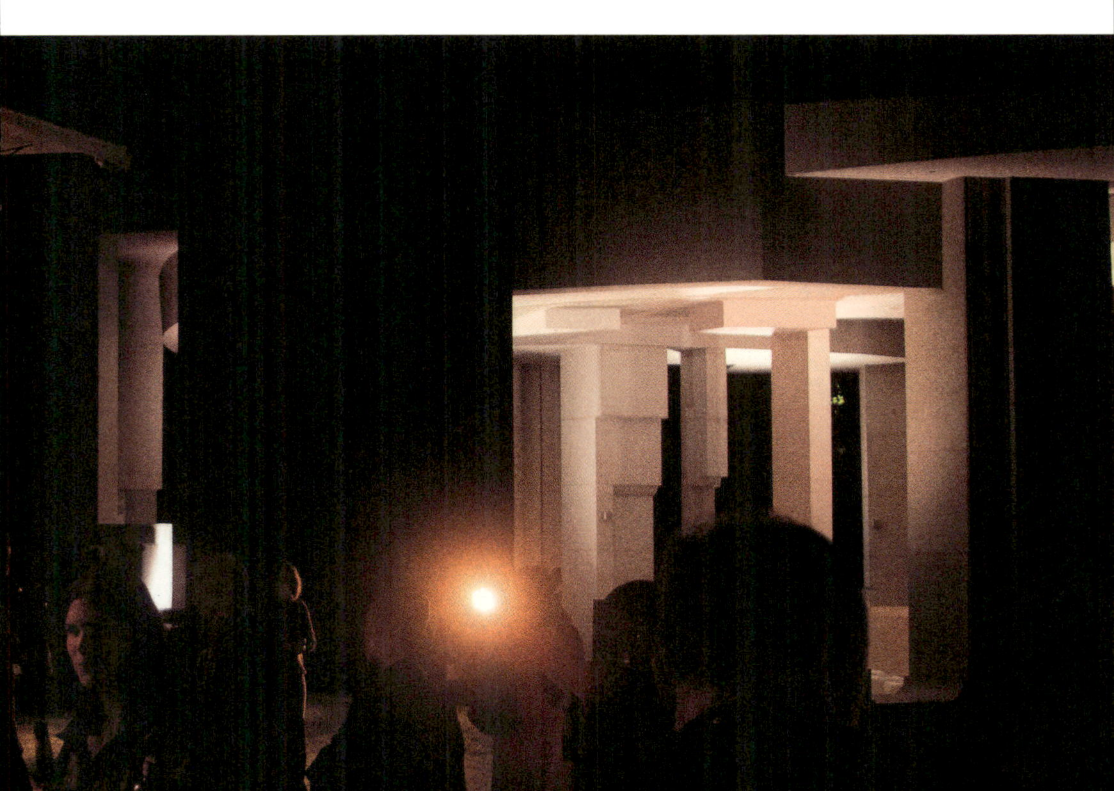

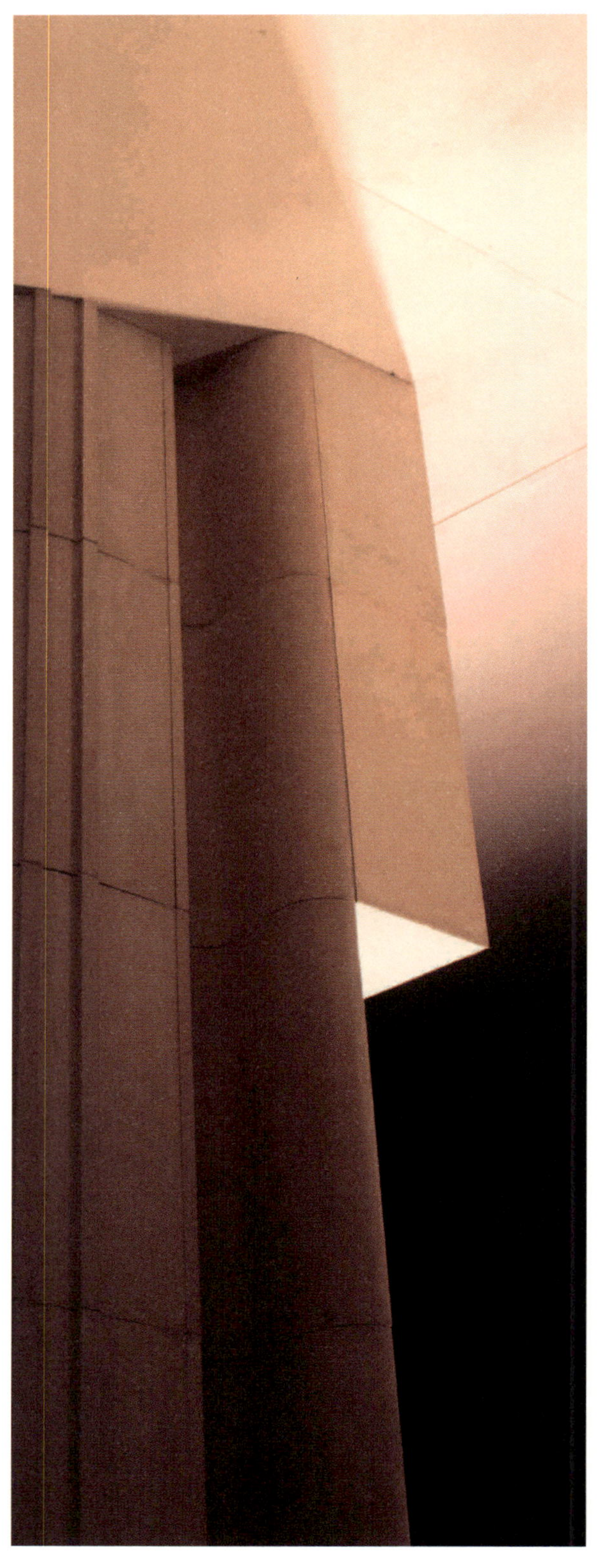

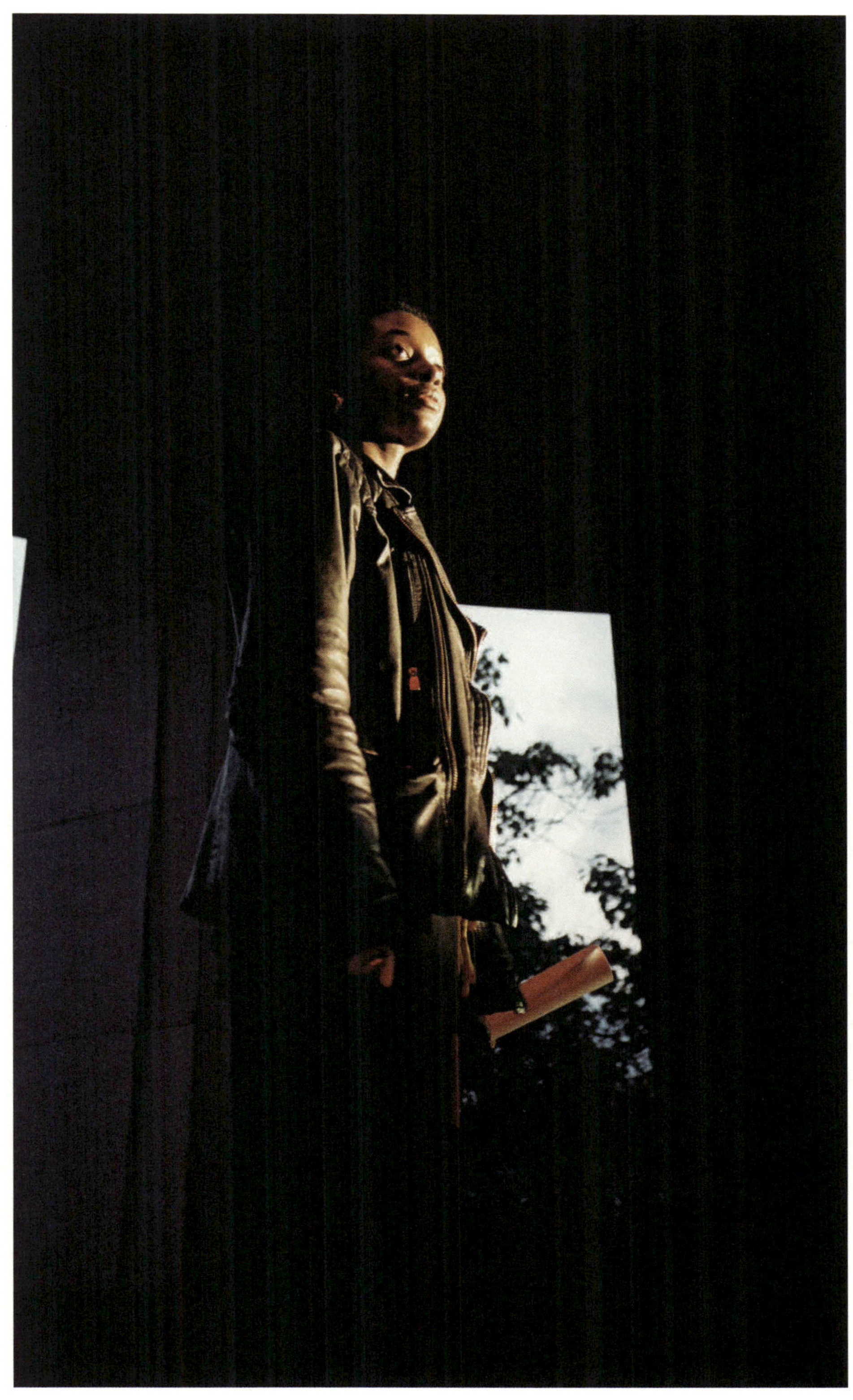

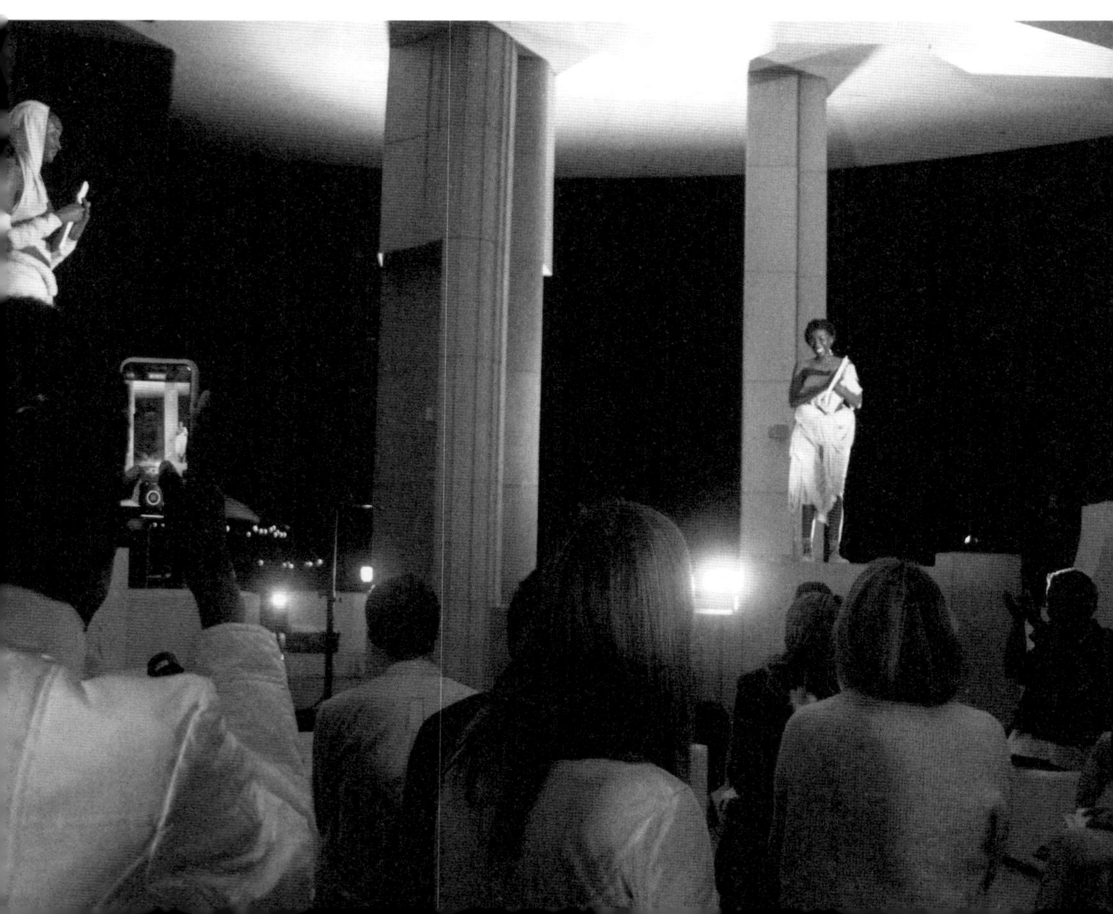

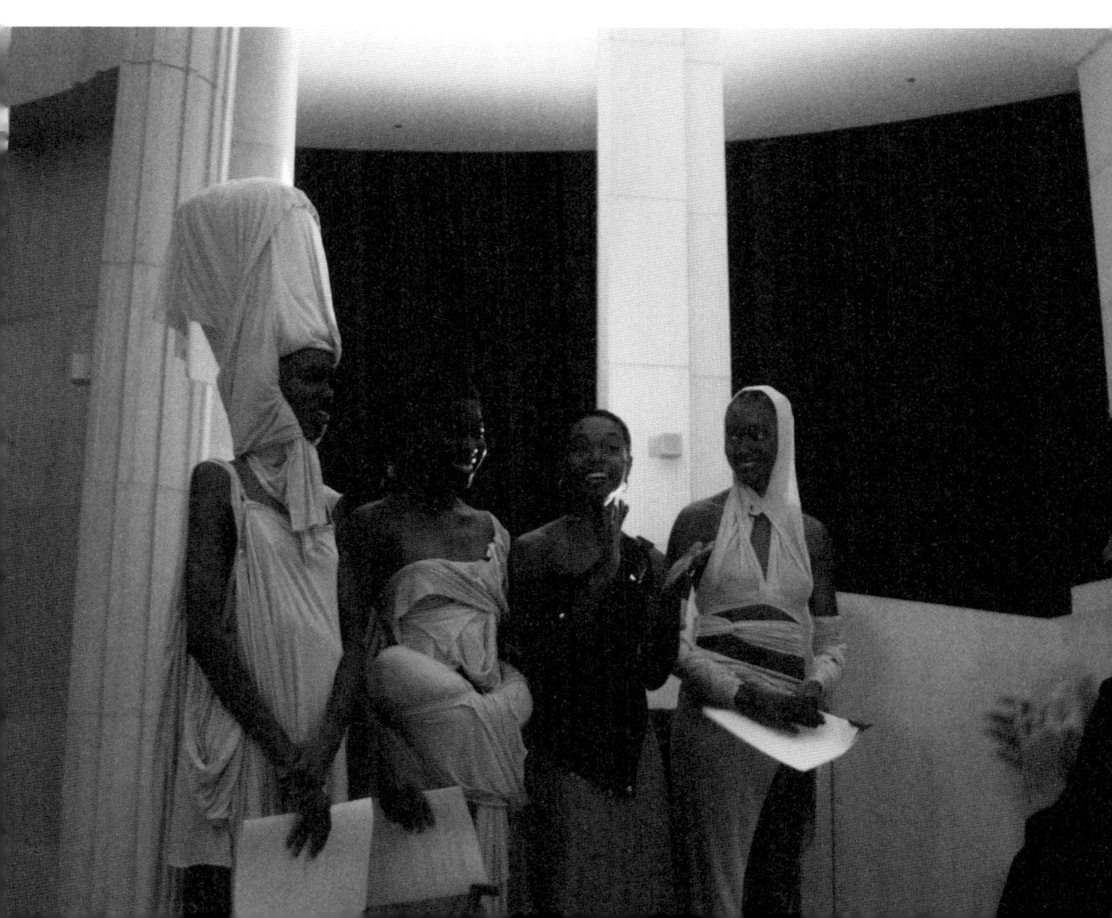

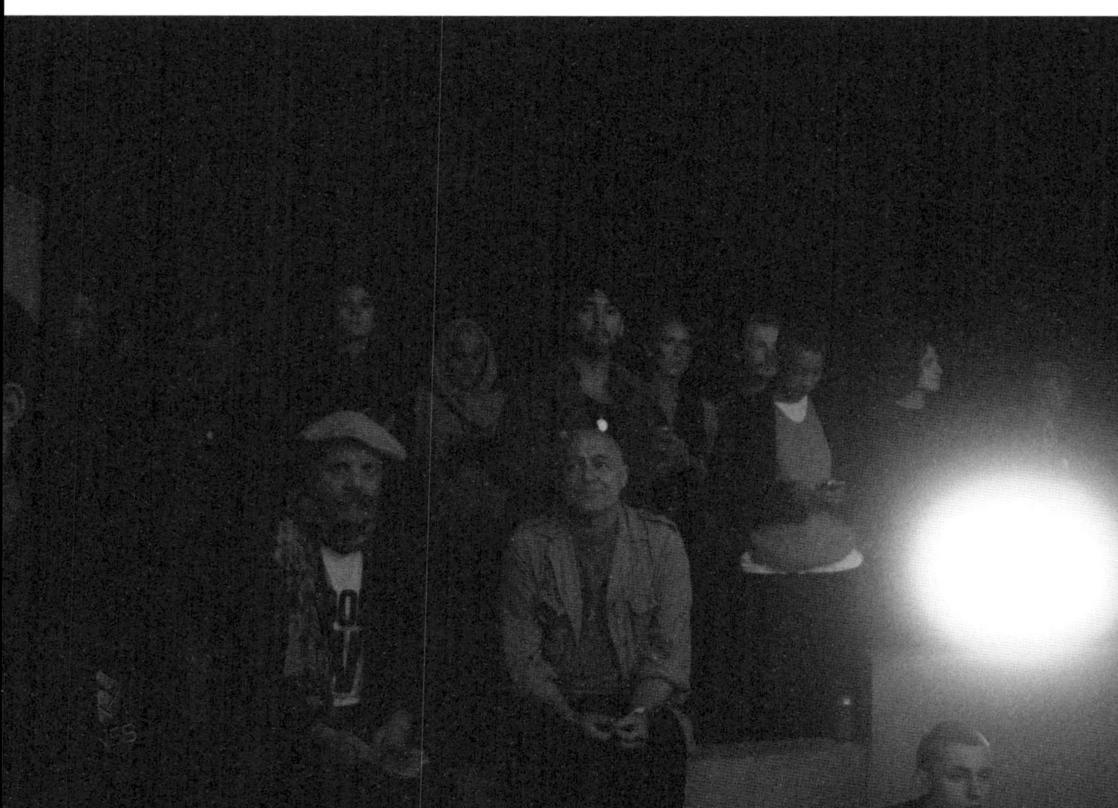

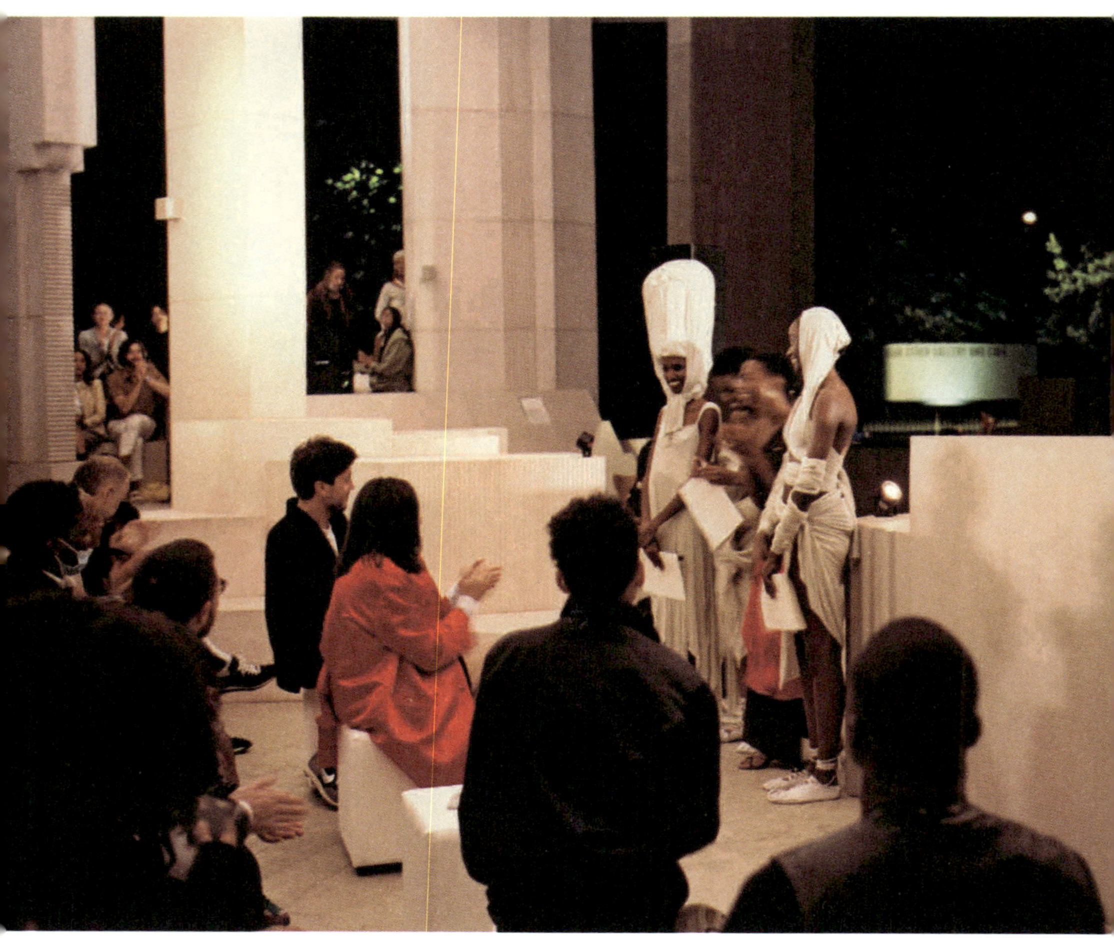

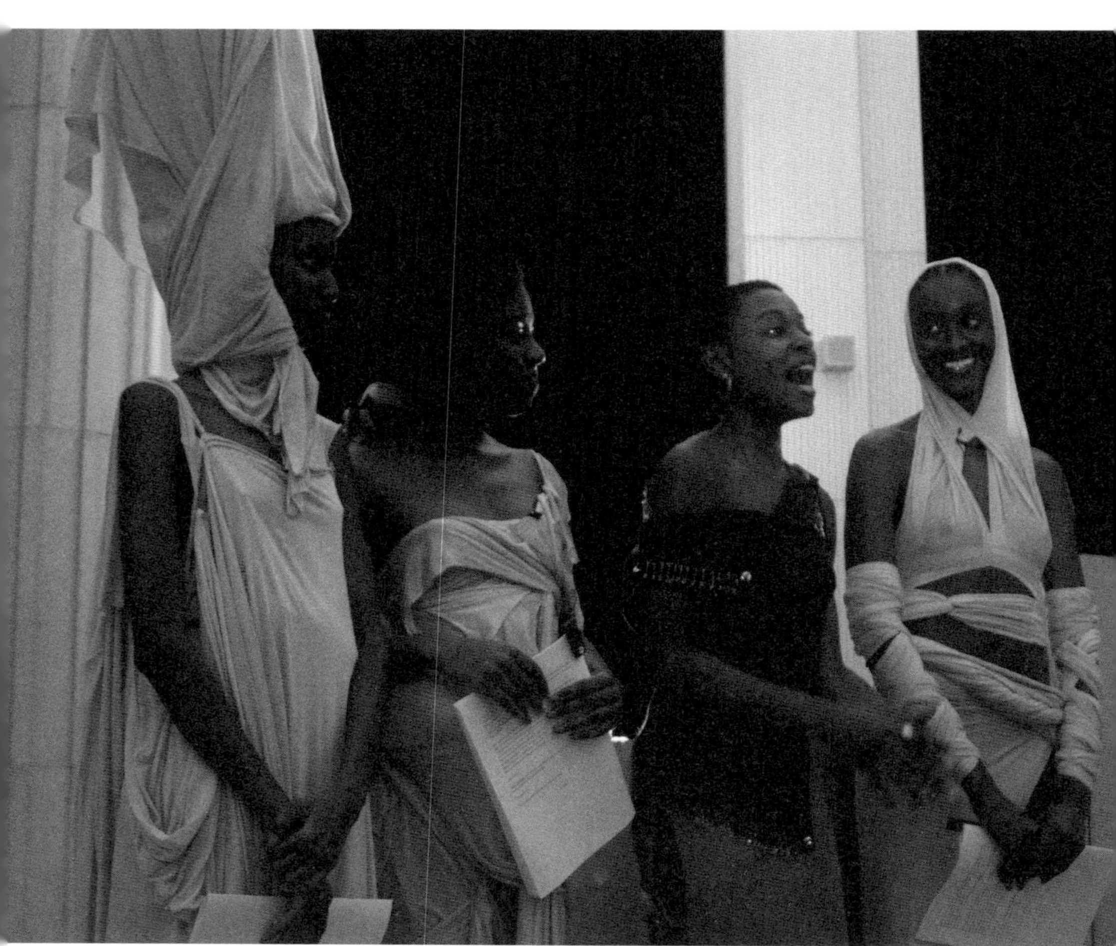

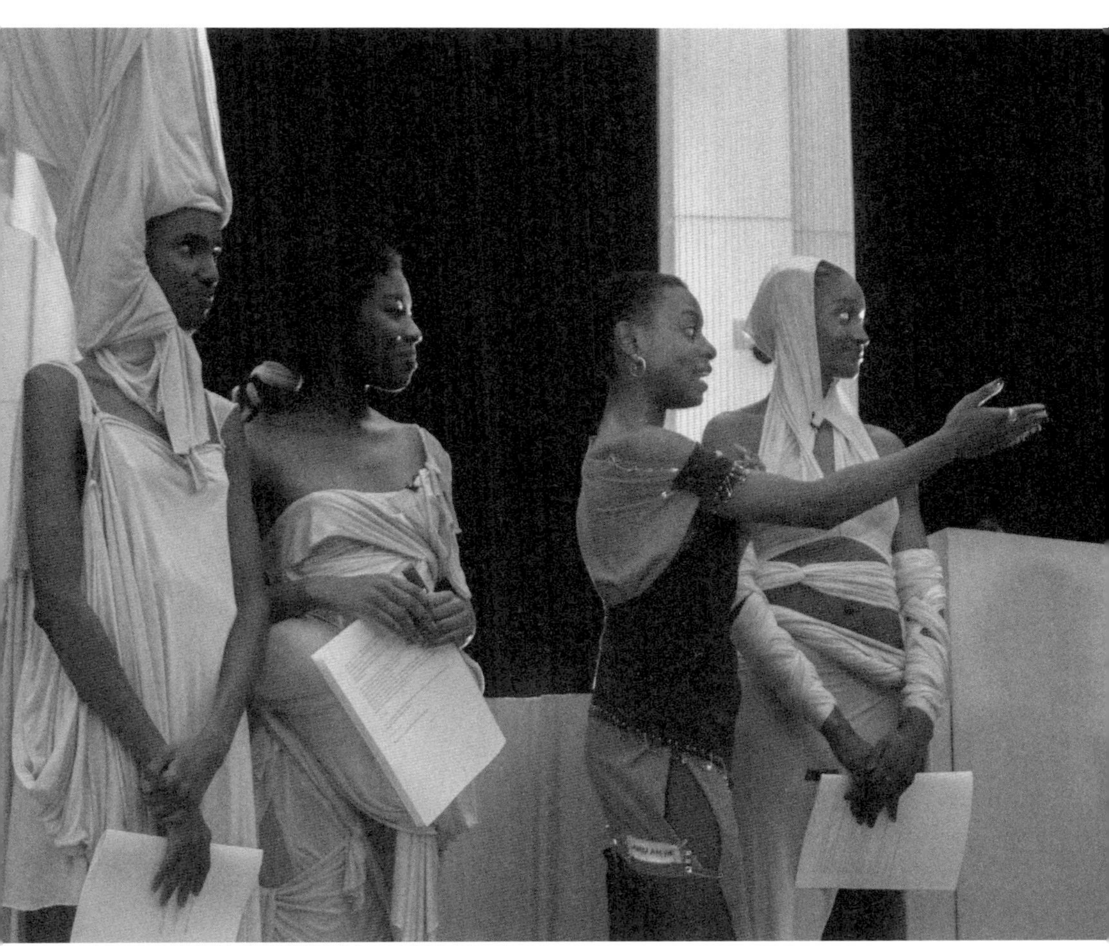

Title page typography by Jonna Mayer

Photography by Henry Jay Kamara
Pages
38-39, 42-43, 46, 52-53, 95, 98-101, 104-105, 110-113, 115-117, 120, 122-125, 128-136, 138-144, 148 and 149

Photography by Rosie Marks
Pages
40-41, 44-45, 47-51, 54-63, 94, 96-97, 102-103, 106, 109, 118-119, 127 and 146

(Photography courtesy of Serpentine Galleries and Rhea Dillon)

We Are Here to Slow Time by © Simone White, from *Dear Angel of Death* (Ugly Duckling Presse, 2018)
Page
65

Rhea Dillon is an artist, writer and poet based in London. Examining and abstracting her intrigue of the ‘rules of representation’ as a device to undermine contemporary Western culture, Dillon questions what constitutes the ontology of Blackness versus the ontic.

Jessica Lynne is a writer, art critic, and co-editor of ARTS.BLACK, an online journal of art criticism.

Simone White is the author of *or, on being the other woman*, 2022; *Dear Angel of Death*, 2018; *Of Being Dispersed*, 2016; and *House Envy of All the World*, 2010. She is Stephen M. Gorn Family Assistant Professor of English at the University of Pennsylvania. White lives in Brooklyn, New York.

Elaine Mitchener MBE is a British Afro-Caribbean vocalist, movement artist and composer working between contemporary/experimental new music, free improvisation and visual art. She is a Wigmore Hall Associate Artist (2021-26); a DAAD Artist-in-Berlin Fellow (2022); and was an exhibiting artist in the British Art Show 9 (2021-22). Elaine is founder of the collective electroacoustic trio The Rolling Calf (with *Jason Yarde* and *Neil Charles*).

Acknowledgements for the performance
Written & Directed by: *Rhea Dillon*
Produced by: *Anastasia Sakoilska*
Orators: *Bibi Adulkadir, Sarah Lusack & Sienna King*
Costume Design by: *Jawara Alleyne*
Sound Direction by: *James William Blades*
Original Composition by: *TWEAKS*

Originally commissioned by Serpentine, 2021.
Serpentine Park Nights 2021 was curated by: Claude Adjil, Curator at Large, and Joseph Constable, Associate Curator, with Caterina Avataneo, Assistant Curator.

For the book the artist would like to thank:
Thanks to Elaine Mitchener and Simone White for being mentors in my research for the opera. For their encouragement and support with thinking, writing and workshopping what a libretto could be - it was a privilege to be in communion for so long. Thank you to Jessica Lynne who I had the pleasure of being in residence with during Summer 2021 and whose critique-with-care thinking makes her the best interlocutor I could have asked for.

Thanks to Clem MacLeod and Caitlin McLoughlin, who make the dynamic *Worms Publishing* team, for giving me the opportunity to bring this opera to the page through every finite detail of my edits. It's been a pleasure throughout.

Thanks to *Languid Hands* and the *Black Cultural Archives* for having me as an artist in residence in October 2020 where the beginning of this research was able to be activated. Thanks to *Arts Council England* and *HOME by Ronan Mckenzie* without whose grants the continued research and writing of the libretto would not have happened.

Thanks to Antonia Marsh and Maddy Whitelaw for your belief and consistent support in all avenues of my practice.

Counterspace, your pavilion was a treat to engage with and inhabit for The Serpentine Park Nights 2021 series. Thanks to The Serpentine's team and staff for offering the space and technical support in presenting this work.

Thank you to my friends who listen and take heed to all my worlds: Kusheda, Eni, Asli, Steve, Mowa, Peter and Beth. Special thank you to my linguistic loving friends who push my appreciation for language by their very existence: Sjournee, Octavia and Mandy.

Published by *Worms Publishing* 2023

Worms Publishing
5 Ropewalk Mews
Middleton Road
E8 4LR
Email: studio@worm-s.com
Web: www.worm-s.com

Edited by *Clem MacLeod*
Designed by *Caitlin McLoughlin*

ISBN: 978-1-3999-4881-4